'A stunning tangle of poetry, 1 ... boundary spaces that both con... and let others in. Prose is sensual and heady, like the b... ...rin when someone touches you.'
— **Anahit Behrooz, author of *BFFs: The Radical Potential of Female Friendship***

'Beautiful, astute and full of love, *Curious Affinities* is a book brimming with poetic brilliance about the ways we exist—in relation to ourselves, others and the world around us. It's an incredible achievement.'
— **Sophie K. Rosa, author of *Radical Intimacy***

'This book will playfully rearrange every particle of your being. Each page sparks and shimmers, tracing bright paths between prose and poetry: deft magic with political backbone and a delicious sense of humour. Chauhan is dissatisfied with the cruel and linear world that neoliberalism offers, generously inviting us into different ways of thinking about our common future. She moves through shared and personal universes, shifting back and forth with equal facility between expansive observations and intimate minutiae of daily life. Whether Chauhan is riffing on jorts-based ontology or unravelling her personal experiences of organising, she constantly refuses one-note answers. Chauhan worlds and re-worlds with gorgeous, resonating complexity.'
— **Pear Nuallak, author of *Pearls from Their Mouth***

CURIOUS
AFFINITIES

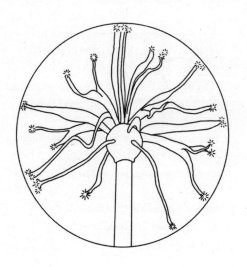

First published in 2023
by Hajar Press C.I.C., London, United Kingdom
www.hajarpress.com
@hajarpress

ISBN 978-1-914221-26-2 Paperback
ISBN 978-1-914221-27-9 EPUB eBook

A Cataloguing-in-Publication data record for this
book is available from the British Library.

Cover and interior art: Han Gunji Stephens
Cover design: Samara Jundi
Typesetting: Laura Jones / lauraflojo.com

Printed and bound in the United Kingdom by
Clays Ltd, Elcograf S.p.A.

CURIOUS AFFINITIES

SOPHIE CHAUHAN

For my loves.

Contents

III / WEAVE

PLAYLIST

Mitski – 'Happy'

Bert Kaempfert – 'A Swingin' Safari'

CAKE – 'Love You Madly'

Donna Summer – 'I Feel Love (12″ Version)'

Deee-Lite – 'Groove Is in the Heart'

The Supremes – 'Baby Love'

Sidney Gish – 'Sophisticated Space'

Queen – 'Cool Cat'

Gourmet – 'Yellow'

Odezenne – 'Bouche à lèvres'

Courtney Barnett – 'City Looks Pretty'

Car Seat Headrest – 'Bodys'

Ball Park Music – 'Alligator'

Karen O – 'Ooo'

Mattiel – 'Keep the Change'

Angel Olsen – 'Spring'

Hop Along – 'Happy to See Me'

The Beach Boys – 'God Only Knows'

Rostam – 'Under Control'

PREFACE

Affinities happen where boundaries meet. With the touching of two exteriors, the promise of transgression and its fierce impossibility come to agonise, tumble and embrace one another. These are the spaces where selves and collectivities are bounded and undone, where all things teem with entanglement and itch to take root in fresh soil. Yet, debris also congeals in our fields of gravity. Treasures are flung into space. Spinning in the orbit of every new connection is the risk of its coming apart.

The following pieces of writing explore different sites and scales of connection and disconnection. They represent an effort to map the vital work we make intimacy do, both in our private lives and in our politics. Proximity, distance, likeness and difference inflect our relations in unexpected and generative ways, especially when it comes to family, race, love, migration, community, class, identity and queerness. We are strung up, pulled apart and stitched back together in the name of common feelings.

But how much difference and distance can intimacy hold? How much proximity and likeness does it require? What learnings can be gleaned from its capacities? And what might we salvage from its limits? These are some of the questions that are braided through this book, albeit in roundabout ways.

As for me, I have lived a very little life, in the scheme of things; the affinities I speak of go to show it. And so, I write from the world I know—equally small—and from my will to stretch it out, to ask you in.

I

THREAD

BACKTALK RODEO

1. Backstory

When Dad was very small, someone told him he was tone-deaf and he never sang again, save two exceptions. The first was at a conference a few years ago, where, fuelled by an open bar and a sense of relative anonymity, he partook in group karaoke on closing night. He claims to recall nothing of the performance beyond his choice of song: 'My Way' by Frank Sinatra. The second exception took place in a dream last October. We are in the car and he sings along to the radio like it's nothing. The voice that my mind invents, that it spins from speech alone, is the most familiar thing I've ever heard.

2. Backbone

The body without organs runs three red lights,
mutters *what the fuck man!* at a Lime scooter hoon,
sighs *I'm home* (without lungs) to the patient dark
that waits up on the first step of many

to the kitchen, where, with shoes off and kettle on,
the mouth (without oesophagus) will wet itself.
To the bathroom, where the outermost of many
skins (without depth) will wet itself, then be dry

in time for bed. The body without organs scales
two more flights. The floorboards groan,

3

unappeased by the caution of tiptoes taken
by the mass (without weight) that climbs

to the top of the house. Where light leaks in from
all sides; where the sound and heat rest after rising.
The body without organs closes windows, latches doors,
says good night to the mirror (without shape),

and lies still. Except the hands that pick each other,
loose confetti on the floor. Or the tinny pulse between what
other bodies know as vertebrae. Or the tumble several surfaces
beneath, the one that makes it known

the stomach would be empty if it had one.

3. Backside

This is disco, baby.
You, me and your dump-truck ass

will writhe like slugs in salt.

Sar, the taste of our beat returns
in times on top of now:

when you arc back round like a chorus
to splash in the puddle of my love;

when my head, in amyl blossom,
thinks to tell you WE'RE GROOVECATS

and you can't help but agree.

As Donna Summer comes to swing
in the hammock of my pelvic floor,

you are smiling with your eyes shut.
I backflip through the smoke,

belly-skin taught, ready now
to fill up on your rhythm.

4. Backpedal

She is knuckles deep and I am drafting a poem. It goes:

> *She is knuckles deep and I am drafting a poem.*

And that's all so far.

5. Backlit

I want to explain what it feels like to be brown and touching
a white lover's back and to be kicked by the sight of it, really. I
would say it's about contrast, and how the articulation of difference in the visual field disrupts its dissolution via the haptic
senses, and how such a disruption is a visceral event. Of course,
it's got to be a little bit about my father's brown hand on my
mother's white back as well, and whatever model that instilled
in me of ideal intimacy. I'm sure there's also something in there
about the lesbian cliché of seeking fusion, and yeah, we merge
from time to time: soft tissues start to fissure, weak from wear.
The thing is, knowing what it's about doesn't change the facts
that my hand is at its brownest when it's on my lover's back, or
that sometimes I want to disappear.

6. Backfire[1]

Having A Tiff With You

is even more keen than the view over San Sebastián, Irún,
    Hendaye, Biarritz, Bayonne
or being sick to my stomach at the Monte Igueldo panoramic
    lookout
partly because in your quiet grief you look like a hotter more
    wounded St. Sebastian
partly because of my love for you, partly because of your love
    for early trains
partly because of the fluorescent lights at the funicular railcar
    ticket office
partly because of the stringency our breath takes on before
    tourists and the Atlantic
it is hard to believe when I'm with you that there can be
    anything as full
as solemn as unpleasantly superlative as luminary when right
    in front of it
in the wet Basque 4 o'clock light we are edging back and forth
    against each other like a stone fogging up its sunglasses

7. Bareback

I undress via Möbius strip-tease.

I undress like a wound.

Still, after paradoxes and copper-stained gauze,

she will fuck me so hard I forget my National Insurance number.

8. Throwback

It's New Year's morning and the weak-kneed daylight is collapsing on Melbourne like an affectionate drunk. My wife lies prostrate on a hardwood floor. I watch her stern face prickle with delight as Sar exorcises her through the unsung medium of live ASMR. By way of whispers, anxiety is coaxed from her thoracic cage and treads the walk of shame across the room. We are ready to go when she springs forth from the bedroom wearing my under-14s state hockey shorts and a grin.

It's a trip day with Lukey and I am here to say *yes.* It dawns on us that the thing about having a job is that when you leave, you owe them nothing, but they owe you money. We spend forty-five minutes dancing circles around the verb *curate.* After ice cream by the beach, I tuck the frequency of light behind my ears for safekeeping and head home. We cook for Sar and trace the tramlines like a stencil to the east, where I move with him like always, his knuckles nestled, the pestle to my mortar, in a way that lets me lean back without falling. I am mile high soaring over hot disgruntled bears when I grasp with both hands what is meant by the line *I can't get enough of you.*

It's November of the winter when I try having nothing twice: first with her, then without. I walk to pick up pizza like it is my destiny. She doesn't like the song in my head because the refrain says *I want to go home.* I like it because when I walk to pick up pizza like it is my destiny, it makes me feel like I'm biting the cold back. We are never quite the same amount of hungry, but in the months before I admit I am allergic to gluten, we eat like that, in perfect symmetry. These are the times I want it all: for her to take my leftovers; for me to steal her jeans. I leave Paris in January with her wishes in my pocket, and she stays behind.

9. Backyard

we sit up to witness the dog's last night on earth

wordless, for the most part

only two and a half heaps of heat

happy to share in conduction

we've gone numb in too many gardens

to let it stop us feeling

when the loudest moon I ever saw

climbed up the brittle dark

when we drove across the country

so I could lose it somewhere gorgeous

there, at the tip of your finger, is the littlest of snails

we watch its small life paint you silver

all the lives I come to grip

leave impressions on my palms

I can't believe it, you and me

come closer

read my fortune

THE MIX

Mixed Feeling

Mum is out of reach. She crosses the street, marches ahead, speaks on the phone, stalks a different aisle of the same super-market. My brothers and I fall into a half-hearted orbit, toying with the edges of her vision. The stretch of space between us is an invitation to play. We are three small children in varied states of boredom/ upset/ energy/ distraction. Now and again, a head-check or a hushed *hurry up!* heave us back into her sway. The memory opens like this, with an unremarkable divide. There is no sign of what is to come; the sky does not turn dark, nor does the room crash into silence. It is a wordless and mundane affair. We are three brown children led through the world in the wake of the white woman who birthed us. In parks/ shop-ping centres/ day-cares/ school corridors, where lengths of burnt grass/ nature strip/ wet tiles/ worn carpets hold us apart, a gap opens up that demands to be closed. She walks ahead, out of reach, when the question comes from nowhere:

How will the world know I'm hers?

The question comes from nowhere but the answer lives in my hands. I run to meet her, to lock my itching little fingers in the sureness of her grip. She stands impatient with an arm outstretched. She is offering more than she knows. Glad to have bested the metres of pavement/ corridor/ linoleum/ shelves that recently rendered our kinship suspect, I wield her hand like a hard-won prize. Our digits knit, our steps conform: we fall into alignment and it says *that's right, now you know.*

It's hard to say how I came to see there was a gap that needed to be closed, but looks and questions all around cemented my concerns:

there—the faintest double take
                    is your mum coming to get you?
our family, a dot-to-dot   rapid-fire racial arithmetic
          are you the nanny?   agile glance from face to face
     Dad, mistaken for an Uber driver (again)
                              paying together or separately?
the German exchange kid looks like her son
                    some kind of Brady Bunch situation
          Mum, waiting on the other side of airport security
where did you get your kids from?   an eyebrow on tiptoes
                                        are you lost?

But Mum is within reach now; there is reassurance in the clasping of a contrast, where the clasping is also its creation. And so I reach. Which is to say: I am relieved and drawn into relief by the proximity of her difference. Which is to say: she is most white and I am most brown in the instant of our touch.

There is a similar scene in your memory: a disappeared parent, an ice-cold revelation in a public place. You are lost and at the mercy of whoever comes to find you. A few minutes pass, perhaps a few more, then the relief of reunion runs like soda through your veins. When a lost child is found (which they most often are), they are claimed like a misplaced coat. The event concludes with twin declarations: *that's my --- !* meets *and that's my --- !* and the balance of belonging is restored. In the flood of emotion that ensues, you stash the fleeting sensation from moments before away beneath layers of flesh. It turns to lead at times in the years that follow: a loved one is late to pick you up, or threatens to leave you behind. However brief, your stint as a lost child still holds a weight, exerts pressure. It is here with you now. It is pulsing.

And so it sits in me (with a twist). When Mum is out of reach but well within sight and there opens a gap that demands to be closed, the ghostly mass of a lost child's dread surges hot against my sternum. There it rests as I trace her hands with fingertips etched in her image. This is dispossession without disappearance: the nearer she is, the starker our difference and the less sense we make in relation. In short, there is no space for a colour line inside a proper family.

This is how it happens that I grow up in the feeling that Mum and I cannot belong to one another, a feeling I know without needing to name. The gap remains, demanding as ever. Later, I choose to jump in.

Mixed Fiction

How do we know where a feeling comes from, what it picks up on its way? As I trawl this sense of dispossession up through the muck of memory, unexpected fragments come floating to the surface. The feeling has its own inheritance. What lives in me in the form of emotion is spun from the substance of colonial power and its effort to make meaning of 'race'. From its pseudo-scientific fabrication to its violent defences in the present, racial difference has been made a material reality through the fictions and forces of empire. The colour line that cleaves apart the bond I share with Mum has taken centuries of dedicated work to sharpen. What motivates this work is not for me to decide. I could suppose that capitalism/ industrialisation/ liberalism/ the Enlightenment/ scientific reason/ or the spectre of 'human nature' built the engine behind Western Europe's race machine, and I do believe that each has played its part. On the other hand, separating the causes and effects of the invention of 'race' would indulge the notion that it serves a single, comprehensible purpose. Insofar as the racial hierarchies have been used to justify colonialism, colonial powers have expended enormous energy to make them appear natural. This paradox—where what appears most natural is produced by the greatest efforts—makes me hesitant to describe the invention of 'race' as a discrete event with coherent consequences.

In fact, perhaps the greatest strength of colonial race thinking is its ability to contain and defend starkly contradictory claims. Early European theories of race are a kind of science fiction; entire worlds have been built on their speculative grounds. Nineteenth- and twentieth-century theorists called upon all sorts of unscientific means to align 'objective truth' with white supremacy. Biologists noted that reproduction among genetically variable plants and animals could create offspring more resilient than their parents ('hybrid vigour'), but so-called interracial reproduction in humans was said to always produce children who were genetically inferior to both parents ('hybrid degeneracy'). The myth of the tragic sterile mulatto and the sickly creole child formed the basis of a 'rational' or even 'humanitarian' argument for anti-miscegenation ideology and law. Contemporary celebrations of mixed-race identity themselves often lean on the principle of 'hybrid vigour', asserting that mixed-race children are physically, emotionally and culturally more resilient than their so-called 'monoracial' peers. Such attempts at anti-anti-miscegenation still feed the farce that racial difference meaningfully corresponds to genetic or even cultural variation.

My experience of mixedness is saturated in the logic of 'hybrid vigour'. Read: (upwardly mobile) Asian man and (higher-classed but lower-salaried) English woman meet, marry, raise (and privately educate) their three brown kids, then move across continents (for some cosmopolitan flair). Our home is almost monocultural and entirely monolingual. Growing up, amidst cries of being *stuck between cultures* or *doubly excluded*,

I hear whispers from people like myself that our burdens will spawn into strengths. Because we belong nowhere, we can venture anywhere. We're the shapeshifting tricksters of a global tomorrow! We aren't ugly ducklings, we're *BEAUTIFUL EURASIAN BABIES*, the soon-to-be uncontested winners of cultural competency training. Whatever racial indignities we face today we will later laugh off as resilience-building rites of passage in the climb toward social ascendency.

Narratives like this enter lives like mine when we feel most in need of reassurance. In this story, being cut off from the people and places that brought you to life makes you the ultimate individual. We enter these stories and become numb to both the pain of lost affinities and the possibility of new connections. *We are not lost, but free.*

Mixed Forces

The fiction of race has always entered and inhabited our bodies by way of feeling. Despite the struggle to keep them separate, the language of anti-miscegenation reveals how scientific reason and embodied emotion converge. The principle of 'racial hygiene' draws from the emotive artillery of disgust, contamination, violation and disease. Likewise, the rhetoric of 'racial purity' conjures comfort, security, goodness, godliness and virtue.

In her work on the political life of 'affect', Sara Ahmed describes emotions as 'sticky' things that pull those who sense them into shared 'economies of feeling'.[2] This is how family lines and colour lines fill up with living people. To be placed along a lucrative family line is to follow a particular trajectory: that which is received shall be passed on in due time. The line is straight and narrow. It points in one direction. Common feelings travel within a stuck-together group and accumulate through movement like the charge of a magnet. The attractive pull of this charge requires the counterforce of repulsion against outside groups. If we think of family lines as the currents along which common feelings flow, racial lines emerge at the group's repellent edge to form borders that cannot be crossed.

Let us briefly see my brown for its specific way of sticking. For most of my life, I am a British settler in so-called Australia with two passports and a great deal of baggage. The brown in which I live left Delhi in 1961 to claim a piece of London's outer west. During the two-generation tenure that it built before my birth, my brown fell from upper caste to working class before commencing its rapid ascent towards wealth. Other browns came before and after—as they did to so-called Australia, where we moved when I was seven—inflecting the shape and purpose of racial logic across the British Empire. Mine is not so different from the 'undifferentiated brown stuff' that George Orwell observes in 1939 on the streets of Marrakech.[3] I do not pass for white, although I am sometimes clocked as mixed. My brown sits close to Dad's brown in the summertime. When the days grow short and it inches away, it's as though I am turning see-through. These days, my atheist and culturally Western brown is hailed by Hindutva recruiters one day and reproached by Islamophobes the next. In short, my brown matters. It has substance/ threat/ contagion/ excess/ doom and history clinging to its surface.

As my brown goes to show, feelings are not the only thing passed around the familial-cum-racial collective, nor the only thing getting stuck. Capital also makes use of these pathways, flowing freely and gathering weight along certain lines over time. This process of motion + time = accumulation is what makes inheritance something that grows as it is passed down family lines. In this way, both the white nuclear family and its scaled-up sibling, 'the white race', are vital technologies of capitalism. Regarding them as such highlights how the selective hardening, policing and severance of family ties have been used to serve colonial power. Produced by the illicit crossings of family and colour lines, the half-caste/ hybrid/ creole/ mongrel/ mulatto/ coloured/ mestizo/ ambiguous/ mixed-race body is teeming with potential energy. Left alone, it could undermine centuries of work put into making racial boundaries appear both absolute and natural. Without a racial logic to organise us into different degrees of humanity, the unequal distribution of property, power and personhood under capitalism simply could not stand.

Within a capitalist system structured around the accumulation of property, ownership and power collapse into one. It comes as no surprise, then, that empire seeks not only to acquire possessions for itself but also to police the property relations of its subjugated others. When ownership is the defining factor of human subjectivity, dispossession is the sharpest tool of dehumanisation. As less-than-human, the colonised cannot claim ownership of themselves, let alone of their children. This strategy of dispossession-as-dehumanisation targets more than the colonised individual's ability to own. In addition, the possibility of possessions being circulated, inherited or accumulated is extinguished through the destruction of family lines. The colonial capture of land, life and labour requires that the kinship systems of colonised people are diced up and rearranged. Children are stolen away in the settler colonies and born into bondage on plantations. Family ties are tugged at and twisted, snapped and unravelled to suit the conditions of exploitation. So the colour line does its cutting.

Mixed Future

Instead of breaking down families like mine, present-day racial capitalism has found canny ways of putting them to use. My type of mixedness keeps cropping up as a symbol of a globalised future. In particular, the (quite literal) marriage of Asian and

European powers represented by families like my own coincides with an increasing will on the part of Western states to integrate growing Asian economies into global capitalist networks. We are everywhere in advertising, 'racially ambiguous' faces here to sell entry into the cosmopolitan class. Our image takes part in the propagation of a dangerous fantasy: one day we will all be mixed and racism will disappear.

If anti-miscegenation thinking makes up part of my cultural inheritance, there is something to be said about the strange celebration of mixedness I swim in today. I can hear this expressed in a chorus around me, although it is painfully hard to locate. A white woman approaches my brother and his white then-girlfriend to say *your kids will have the perfect skin colour.* People coo at a stranger's baby: *what a lovely mix!* Interracial relationships and mixed-race people are not new in any way, yet they have come to represent a future where racism (read: white guilt and discomfort) is dissolved by good feeling.

I think of my parents and what they must have made of the ripples surrounding their romance. Was there a thrill in the illicit? A sense of self-righteousness? Mum doesn't have much to say on the matter, other than that in cultural terms *Dad is practically white.* Their romance carries the air of London in the '90s, of a generation eager to turn a blind eye to race in the name of transcendent love. For Dad, it's simpler: *opposites attract.* We were born out of magnetism. We were current.

While the type of mixedness heralded by the multicultural mainstream is separated from whiteness by colour, it is almost indistinct in terms of class, culture and political vision. This is especially true when we consider the ideal of 'transcending' race that mixed families are supposed to inhabit. What does it mean to aspire to a life unmarked by race? From an anti-racist perspective, this would mean the end of racialisation altogether. But from the popular stance of the not-quite-white, it is closer to seeking escape. This looks like a politics of meritocracy/ *get over it/* neoliberalism/ *why does everything have to be about race* and 'model minority' complicity that both denies the persistence of racial violence and blames its victims for having failed to 'transcend'.

The worst part is that it doesn't even work. Attachment to Mum gives the rest of my family very little in her absence. Loving whiteness, being born out of whiteness, chasing its pipe dreams and being raised in its peripheries can only offer so much shelter. Colour lines are just as real for those living at their borders.

Mixed Frequencies

I have tried to map the substance of a complex feeling. The colonial world has spun fictions, gathered forces and imagined futures to keep me from belonging to my mother, to keep her from belonging to me. Between us is a gap that cannot be closed but that is filling up all of the time. It's hard to say how much of our relationship has been touched by disconnect. Perhaps the strangest thing about the feeling of dispossession I have described is that it has never been reciprocated. To her, my brothers and I were always just her children—nothing more, nothing less—and the instances where strangers called our kinship into question always came as a shock. In the tight cram of maternal intimacy, there was never room for race. Mum is perhaps the only white person in the world capable of not 'seeing' my brown, which sounds impossible but is something that I know to be true. It makes sense in retrospect that the period of greatest friction between us came as I began to speak openly and critically about race in our family. I doubled down on the divide she had successfully 'transcended'; in doing so, I became the agent of dispossession, with race as my weapon of choice.

There were countless other factors at play that stirred tension between us over the years, but I can't help but think that part of me was driven to restore a balance: if she couldn't be mine, why should I be hers? I needed her to know that what separated us was absolute, that there was a brutality in the pretence that she could ever know or understand me. I needed her to recognise the gap before I could reach out in good faith. When she did, the language came in pieces. I had been interviewing other mixed-race Asians with white mothers for a research project, and I spoke with Mum about the bizarre patterns that showed up. To my surprise, she agreed enthusiastically with what I had to say. Hearing that the same misrecognitions occur in other relationships like ours emboldened both of us to talk about how we did and did not learn to see each other. Practice and, funnily enough, physical distance eased these conversations along. Where unbelonging once felt like the endpoint of our relationship, it started to feel like an opening. *If you can't be mine, what else can you be?*

It strikes me how much the language of possession shapes how we talk about wellbeing/ connection/ immersion/ support/ home/ safety and love. *This is where we belong. I have you. I want to be yours.* Everything that grounds us in the world and connects us to each other is confined to a grammar made for property. This is not a wholesale wrong, and there is much to be said about the value that relations framed this way add to our lives. At the same time, the lexicon of relational belonging reflects a worldview responsible for shattering kinship structures in service to racial capital—a material process of violence that still injures and haunts so many. I think about what it means for the logic of ownership to have tethered itself to our very sense of humanity so that dispossession could become dehumanisation. We learn that we need to *have* and not just to *be with*, because if we cannot lay claim to another we are nothing ourselves. But other ways of living are not unimaginable; in fact, very little of our world is properly fixed in the trappings of capitalist culture and its racist motivations. Love without likeness, curiosity without comprehension and attachment without ownership can all fit within a family.

For me and Mum, at the very least, not fully belonging to one another has been cause for both hurt and hope: hurt because we have both felt loss, and hope that what we lost was never really worth having. These days things are good. My younger self would be outraged by how much we now have in common, by how highly I value her advice. I catch my habits echoing hers. We speak to each other (with minor delays) across a gap that now spans half the world. I hold her on the line and a pixellated answer gently takes form in my hand. The tether is electric. We are close.

CALENDAR

10/8

Faggotry, or else
whatever it is that says
go on, get up there!

11/8

She notes down new words
that I might fancy letting
off-leash in my mouth.

15/8

Warm enough hands will
spring dirt wherever they go.
Come, let's make a mess.

1/9

Sprint or marathon,
our gobs run a tandem race.
Where's the finish line?

4/9

On the train and in
the sky, I dream of a bed
to break my back in.

8/9

Liz kicks the bucket
and we wish in vain for a
singular feeling.

16/9

Bright lights in a shop
full of shit urge me to go
eat a vegetable.

20/9

Strung up tight between
two feelings, now pick: malaise
or melancholy?

26/9

The left back pocket
is near nine months up the duff
with library cards.

24/10

East End on fire
for Diwali, Rishi and
his working-class friends.

12/11

Light from a closer-
than-usual sky holds us,
salt-skinned and giddy.

5/12

The floor is twice clean,
the bedsheets feign to dry and
the page watches back.

14/1

First in line for the
second queue, I see the star,
plain, arrive at work.

YELLOW

for Dad

Paul Simon's 'Graceland' hits the tarmac like
a Thursday morning hallelujah, all jank and
nameless choristers, bold as jammy yolks.
I know the album front to front; the rear
end rings out after I am dropped off—off he
reels, unsinging, to another kind of reverie.

On a drive through the middle of France, under
the scrutiny of a sunflower jury, I am back with
my head in his hands, pleading guilty to leaving
like we tend to. The inevitable blows in on an
icterine breeze, humming hot between our chests.
A little of his yellow rubs off as we part ways.

He is front-garden marigold pride and joy on
the day of his second wedding. He is stained up to
the neck like a well-loved wooden spoon.
He is papa bear tummy rub with a slice of lemon
meringue pie, the right parts sweet and sour, the
bite of fickle coffee from his cadmium machine.
He is buttercup gleaming in Brasil [sic] football kit.
He is buttered-up crumpet and banana ice cream.
He is bow-legged bundle, the colour of surprise.

I sport his dead mother's under-floorboard gold
like a brown boy who worships Drake and rides
the wings of Nike to weekend maths tuition.
Her hoop, chain and pinkie ring scat the
dot-to-dot lines of my left-side body. He spots
them without speaking. He tries to listen in.

Once, we rummaged through end credits to
wrench free the name of an insurance ad song
like a missing part quarried from a junk drawer.
He holds one hand like a weapon over *play* and
shoots. We are both trigger-happy. The flute-light
melody fires away, the target a duckling-down smile.

Of course, he understands better than us why
the sun is most yellow when brought to its knees.
Who knew the atmosphere could be so generous
as to scatter the best bits, to press them on evening
skin? We are to one another only part-refracted
sky. Some lives glow aureolin at the limits.

ROOFTOP

Generational time has too much punctuation. I'm looking for the bowed gait of a man who keeps on getting shorter. I'm looking on, where he is walking, and waiting for him to turn round. We wade through a crowd of millions, an oceanic range of knock-off trainers. He traverses a Tetris traffic jam that rearranges itself in slow motion after him. There's a shortcut on the other side of Red Fort, he insists. Right behind him I am feeling the tourist I am. He obviously does not realise, or does not care. The streets close in as if guarding his secret: the fastest way home kept under wraps. It's an unexpected quiet; it seems, like us, to follow a hidden route. A flurry of men on mopeds pass through the still heat, kicking up dust and faint suspicion with their tyres. Ahead, the old man veers around a corner. I think about the pavement, about his level of trust in where he is going. It takes a shout to trip him up. A middle-aged man stands on the curb, stirring his vat of boiling syrup, milk dumpling whirlpool, with a ladle the length of his arm. The shout is a name—the old man's name—a name I neither call him nor ever hear him called. A few words are exchanged in familiar tones before the stranger hands us each a sweet, and we proceed to eat them.

A block away is his childhood home. We climb to the fourth-floor apartment and stand on the roof overlooking the street. He is set against a pale-blue wash. He hasn't got much to say. Despite the cough it fixes in his throat, the atmosphere makes him look young again, like someone I don't know. Fifty years cleave him from this place. Imagine that. Before he was an old man, the old man was a child of his times. We are close to where he went to see the new nation's last rites, his father resolute in staying home. His mother would bring him milk still warm from the buffalo in the front yard. On special occasions, they travelled together on a wagon to visit family in what was then a mud-hut village and is now an industrial annex scuffing the old city's petticoats. He has seen heads fall to the ground over grocery shopping and taken note of how they bounced. In moments of brutal transparency, over burnt cappuccinos in the suburbs of Melbourne, he has told me of the floodwaters that washed the city clean that year, that carried bodies with them. Some Rivers of Blood are not metaphorical. He says: *sometimes nature knows*.

From the rooftop, I watch the world below and inhale the welcome calm. Time is passing all around. Layers of the barest life stack up beneath our feet, keeping us here at this height, raised, exactly where we are. I turn to him and see many men at once, some of whom I love, some of whom I recognise. I turn to him and wait. We leave when he is ready to go.

PHENOMENOLOGY

mouth feel of a diaspora poem:

- a hard-to-bite word
- the tongue, unruly
- something unsayable
- something quoted + italicised
- the texture of humidity
- unsavoury poetic licence
- a numbing but globally available spice
- the juice of a regionally specific fruit
- the outline of another language
- [untranslated/untranslatable]
- a lexical gap-tooth
- a border
- something unsaid
- something stolen
- sibilance
- gum disease
- a pout
- a plosive
- outrage (bitter)
- outrage (sweet)

ass feel of a diaspora poem:

does your grandmother/
        grandfather/
               parent/relation/
                        ancestor/motherland   know

     that every time they tell you a story

          you are mining it for poems?

lung feel of a diaspora poem:

  his hometown gives you all the same cough.

foot feel of a diaspora poem:

where are the feet now?
whose dirt do they kick up
     and how much of it?

are they bedazzled?
are there little hairs on the toes?
can you go walking on a memory?
     which shoes would you wear?

what makes the toes curl? are there blisters?
     does anybody touch them?

     do they smell like other places?
can you smell them from here?

how many layers between them and the earth?
       how many layers between you and them?

are they flat? do they tickle?
       do you let them out off-leash?

       do they have places to be?
do they know where you've taken them?
do they know where they are?
       do you know?
do you remind them?

when a diaspora poem has a foot feel
       do you feel more or less at home?

blood feel of a diaspora poem:

thanks to your parents' unbridled and unsuspecting wonder at the marvels of modern technology, Ancestry.com now owns the rights to your entire genetic code.

head feel of a diaspora poem:

the hybrids trade in
bastardised Morse

  (hyphen-dash
    neither/nor—both/and)

on the hunt for a bargain at
the marketplace of ideas,

tap-slashing trestle tables
in hailstorm negotiations

like myna bird mimics,
like sparkle-famished magpies.

today, the generative power of
dismemberment is white hot, and

real estate near the in-between
is in record high demand.

at close of business, all the happy
punters will pulse toward the exit

with freshly doubled faces
and poems in their tote bags.

bone feel of a diaspora poem:

sensing that you cannot ask the living for details, you go trawling through hotly digitised public records to find out more about what happened to her. when you land on the Hammersmith and Fulham births, deaths and marriages registry, autofill conjures your name in the search bar, like it knows how you feel about gaps.

tail feel of a diaspora poem:

facts are facts, and when a monkey opens a bottle of water
with its mini monkey hands, which are so much like yours,
you're like, fuck, we are really all just monkeys, monkeying
around, eating each other's lice and intimidating tourists—
in which case why not be open for monkey business? you
resolve to eat more bananas and pick up fallen objects
with your toes, to carry yourself with the swagger and style
of a monkey in command, and fuck it, why not make some
monkey noises while you're at it, just for fun! it is time to
demystify your likeness to monkeys, starting with your idea
of human evolution. this is easy when you have a family
of monkeys before you doing monkey family things: monkey
babies and monkey parents, playing, fighting, feeding and
hanging out. for simple comparison, you have in your head a
perfect image of your hands, wet at a child-height sink, and
swapping coloured pencils, and tracing new words, and what
are those hands if not monkey-like, if not small, brown and
curious? you recall your younger brother's puerile grin, his
luminous giggle, his loveable love of general tomfoolery, and
are swept away by how thoroughly, how indisputably he was
a cheeky little monkey for years on end! last but not least,
when it comes to the intergenerational aspect, to the matter
of social reproduction, well, the first film your father saw at
the cinema, which you then watched over and over as kids,
was Walt Disney's *The Jungle Book*, featuring the most racially
inappropriate jazz-playing primate to ever grace the silver
screen (on the good old-fashioned mouth-trumpet), and
hell, if King Louis the orangutan can learn to be like someone
like you, then why can't it go both ways?

heart feel of a diaspora poem:

in choosing to believe that an
even number of elephants is the
key to a balanced life

better judgement succumbs to
brilliant salesmanship:

you buy a second miniature for the mantle
and pretend she would have done the same.

VIRTUAL

in April I dream a disappearance/ LCD/
lowest common denominator/

the battery life runs out like toothpaste/
we squeeze until it's gone/

I tickle the figment/ metal cooling in my hands/
frozen at the interface/

it hurts but I still make you/
I make you all the time/

this little weight comes everywhere/ a pinkie indent/
a pocket hole/

flat against the back/ in the sheen of keys more tapped/
and there you are/

dogs at your feet/ swimming in dinner noise/
forehead blue in TV light/

you take your teeth out for the night/
and show me gums/

as snails crisscross the windowsill/
we theorise a family: big medium & small/

in motion without moving/ every sacred pixel/
hard to believe/

I kneel to scrape a crisscross off the carpet/
still wet/ the culprit missing/

with a hotness by my side/ an unrelenting moon/
inches up the black/

brings the whole Atlantic with her/ sets us down/

the gulls here sing a song I hardly know/ and/

play by play/ my head bikes to your house/ thinking/

how vital/ to know the underbelly of your chin/

to know you were up all through my night/ come morning/

the thinnest veil of dreams/ will make its bed/

on top of mine.

II

KNOT

DYKES!

Dykes are on their way, jangling like nothing else. Dykes put four on the floor and make mayhem with their hips. Dykes are at the library learning about dykes: who they were, who they seek to become. Dykes in school uniform shout from the bus stop *I like your hair I love your jeans you guys are cool*—and sometimes just *DYKES!* We turn back and see dykes like us, faces falling open like fists gone to sleep. Dykes are everywhere, sort of.

We were plenty of things before we were dykes. We are plenty of things still. We are more + less + sometimes other than dykes. Being a dyke is never just being a dyke. It has to be knowing a dyke + loving a dyke + touching a dyke + remembering a dyke + imagining a dyke who is yet to exist. To be a dyke is to do a dyke's laundry, to sweep up the confetti of a freshly freshened fade. Dykes live in the search for rings fallen from bedside tables, in a chorus of dyke drama + dyke discourse + dyke disaster + dyke debauchery.

To be a dyke is to love being a dyke, sometimes. Dyke love knows how to touch me, when not to touch me, when to lie still + what to say. We are in the business + pleasure of being dykes for ourselves + for one another. When I am in the presence of dykes, when I am in the tight pocket of dyke love, that is when I am most serene. So it helps that dykes find each other. In school plays + lecture halls + locker rooms + anon message boards + workshops + queues + familiar streets + less familiar streets, dykes find each other. Dykes smell + hear + taste + summon + transform + challenge + defeat other dykes. Our glances stick together despite efforts to gloss by.

Just as we were plenty of things before we were dykes, so

dykes varied among themselves before we entered the fold. Dykes have been a class: blue-collar workers graced by the absence of men. Dykes have been butch + femme + studs + married + divorced + mothers + daughters + secrets + workers + gender traitors. Dykes have been impotent + dangerous + criminal + crazy + even sometimes unremarkable. Insofar as dykes were all of these things, so they remain today. Dykes are threats + anomalies + failures + miracles. We are the destinies + accidents of the cultures from which we emerge. Dykes are trans + queer + genderless + overflowing with gender, and all the time we are dykes. Dykes don't make sense, but we are always making. Dykes make love + make money + make meaning + make do + make it good + sweet to be dykes.

When my dyke lover says to me *how incredible, how unlikely, how inconceivably wonderful it is that I am a dyke + you are a dyke + we are in love,* I know exactly what she means. We didn't have to be dykes. It wasn't even probable. To not only be a lesbian in love with a woman but be a dyke in love with a dyke is to exceed. And so we have so much to share. And so I permit her repetition, her unceasing awe at the fact of our being dykes and in love, because I too am grateful. Holding the excess of being a dyke is no mean feat for us both.

Among dykes who love dykes + who love being dykes, the bounty we collect is an opening. We think *here is our chance at unity, here is a moment of grace.* The promise of 'just dyke-ness' lets us forget that we are dykes in and against finite bodies + racial orders + classed limits. But dykes are born + raised + taught + supported + betrayed + enabled + contained in as many different ways as there are different ways of being a dyke. And so at the checkout + under dry ice + through liquid displays + on pages of history where I see dykes who are like me but not, I want to say *how incredible, how unlikely, how inconceivably wonderful that I am a dyke + you are a dyke + I love you*

+ we will never be the same.

CONTRAST

Afternoon sun leaves its lipstick on my cheeks. The mark greets me in the mirror with a wink. I start, a little flustered by the badge of lewd affection I have been both flaunting and forgetting all day. There is something bold and rushed about its arrival. I brown the way others bruise, with unexpected haste. Staring out from inside the dark, I wonder after its staying power. The kiss can be like water on concrete, a ghost that soaks away. It can also settle, sedimentary, unseen until it's stuck. If Mum saw it, she'd say *you've caught the sun*—as though someone had cried *go long!* or I had taken to casting lines into the sky. The shock of all that brown in the mirror starts to shrink as I settle into mutual rapture with the heat. I wear the signs of summer loving with the brazenness they merit, but showy affairs don't tend to last. The cool change comes to butter my fingers and snip holes in all my nets. If radiation on the skin is an accretive force, the winter strips me down. I descend along a gradient until the raw stuff of a surviving body starts to show through. I see passages of blood; my bones approach the surface. Reflected against white tiles, under brutal fluorescent lights, my skin will run flat for the season. Every year, a brand-new disappearance.

The art of representing the multicultural ideal is a bit like quilting; the parts have to tessellate so that no two like colours touch. Both require cautious mathematics to work out the bare minimum and reasonable maximum of differences that can be stitched together. In my social life, I am an accent flush on a patchwork of variegated beiges, which is to say I make my group of friends easier to photograph. The image of us side by side is worth more than the sum of its parts. Aren't we a handsome bunch, knit together, grinning for the ages? The curated range of skin tones and dungarees has us looking like the cast of *Sesame Street*. As part of such ensembles, I follow myself in two dimensions, shoulders raised, arms around a loved one or a stranger. The pictures make it onto website headers and Instagram ads. Even when I'm not in them, I can spot my mid-brown, racially ambiguous gender-fucked counterpart in any given multi-culti line-up. Our representation is so ubiquitous that my friends and I will never really own our own togetherness. So why not lean in? Let's be traders in the currency of contrast. Let's get rich!

Everyone has a picture from the Flinders Street Station photo booth. It's a strange rite of passage for Melbourne's fast friends and young lovers. For six dollars you can make your debut, three ways enamoured in glossy black and white. Teenage bedrooms wear those strips like decorated soldiers. You'll find them strewn across the city, pinned up with fairy lights and missing after breakups. Naturally, I couldn't wait to have one of my own; when my new best friend, casual as ever, suggests that we christen our courtship with headshots, I struggle hard to keep my cool. We plot our poses in advance, squeeze into the curtained cabin and push coins down a hungry slot. After three frenzied flashes it spits us back. We hunch round the printout to see. Sar's face is mapped in all its contours, shining bright beneath a rain of dark curls. Next to her is an assortment of teeth, sclera and forehead shine arranged on a charcoal smear. I am nowhere to be seen. The true vintage charm (and primitive photochemical technology) that makes this booth a destination wears off without a word. My best friend keeps the picture and

I don't ask for a copy.

How do white dyke couples go about deciding who gets to have a blonde bowl cut and who has to remain a middle-parted brunette? I imagine them drawing up time-share agreements and plotting transitions on the calendar, brainstorming distinctive features to try on with the seasons. I realise why being assumed to be affectionate relatives rather than lovers leaves lesbians embittered. Still, a lot of you aren't doing yourselves any favours. I'm glad I get to dress like my girlfriend without our looking too alike. In fact, we only get the sisters question once, and it comes from a conman chimney sweep, so there isn't much room for indignance. The guy is white, in his thirties and exactly as charming as someone in his dual line of work ought to be. We gather behind to watch him coax clumps of filth down the flute and into the bedroom fireplace. As he turns around, his inquisitive looks bounce off me (sitting), her (standing), the decor (homosexual) and the dust heap (impressive) before he reaches his conclusion: 'cohabiting siblings'. Riding high on the novelty of the visit (and oblivious to the extortionate bill he will soon make us pay on the spot), we take his remarks with uncharacteristic good humour. We don't even say what we are to one another. We just laugh, swap looks and tell him *no*.

I shut one eye at a time to see her better. Left, and right, and left: two lines of sight, two inches apart. I meet her gaze. The contact is closer with the vision split in half, but I take my time shifting gears. Mechanical whirs and twitches pull her in and out of focus. I double her on purpose just to reconcile her edges. Then her aperture declines. Dusk enters the room like the mother of sleeping children, gentle and quick. We lie still, secretly awake, and wait for daylight's door to close. The coast is clear so we dip our toes in the wet dark left behind. No one will see the mess until morning. For now, I blur and she gleams.

Despite efforts by an administrator to knock the feminising *e* off her name on the invitation, my high-school girlfriend makes it to my Year Eleven formal. It's a nervous occasion. No one has said to us that she is not allowed to attend, but no one has given permission either. She turns up pale, blonde and tense in a black suit with an origami corsage. I am dress-clad and struggling to walk. We gather at my friend's place first to watch everyone else get tipsy and gawk at my classmate's much, much older boyfriend. The host's mother busies herself topping up prosecco and taking poorly lit pictures. My parents—immune to the thrills of both staged coming-of-age events and underage drinking—stand around looking bored. Against the displays of unbridled enthusiasm, I can't help but feel hurt that they don't ask for a photo with me and my girlfriend. My friend's mum takes one anyway. It comes out terribly, the collective discomfort palpable, but I'm glad for the attention nonetheless. She then moves on to couple shots. I don't know who hears her comments as she comes to take ours. If they do, I don't know what they make of it. Squinting through the lens to frame us just right, she rules us picture-perfect. *Aren't you two stunning! The contrast …*

Can anyone tell me what it means to be *of colour*? Because I would tell you that it doesn't mean much. To the extent that

44

it is meaningful (read: politically useful) to shepherd everyone and everything that is not white into a single collective, you might as well name your racial logic and say *non-white*. Some people will say that categorical *non*-ness centres its partnered term. I say fuck it, maybe whiteness is at the centre of how we think about race. Maybe it's the sharpest line in the sand. We point to it with eyes averted. Which is to say that *of colour* is as tethered to whiteness as *non-white* is. Maybe it's just easier to say. And then what about the shuffle of syntax, the subtle rearrangement that says we are now drawn from colour rather than marked by it? Some old words don't want to be new. If I am *coloured*, I am subjected to a process. I am talking about an act of colouring in—an act that has an agent, has an object, that happens over time. Maybe *colour* is a happening, active, not passive. I do it to myself and have it done to me. How can I be *of* it? For that to be, *colour* would have to take ontological priority. I would be *colour*'s derivative. But there is no *colour* before, not really. There is us and all our brown; there are lines drawn in the sand. There is life, so keen to know itself it studies how to kill.

In my head there are brown hands on a white body. In her head there are white hands on a brown body. In both of our heads there are things that this could mean. In neither of our heads are there helpful things to say about them. In my hands and body there are nerve endings that are touched as well as touching. In her hands and body there are nerve endings that touch everything that touches them. In the gaudy pink steam, the difference between touching and being touched starts to dissolve. I lean across the bath and kiss my own knee.

The gag works for two reasons. First, in its own slapstick paradox, colour-blind ideology turns every case of organic interracial intimacy into a spectacle. Second, except at greetings and disasters, I've never been a touchy friend. Making a habit of crossing platonic colour lines would spoil the chance to make contact obscene. And that's exactly what we do. A white arm brushes mine and I make us stop to acknowledge that *we did it*, that *racism is over*. My oldest friend, drunk and inspired, weaves each of her fingers between my bare toes and gasps at the thrill of having *finally ended it all*. When I'm feeling particularly post-racial, the dog placing a needy paw on my knee is enough to set off tearful celebrations. Each joke makes a mockery of stock-image multiculturalism but also quietly assures me that both of us are noticing, that it's not just me who sees. Our circus hugs a kernel of truth: it's a burden and a treat to be spectacular.

MARRIAGE STORY

9 August 2017

The Marriage Act 1961 enshrines 'the union of a man and a woman to the exclusion of all others' as the Australian paradigm of love. Some people want to see this change, but the Conservative parliamentary majority decides that before the government can legalise same-sex marriage, the Australian Bureau of Statistics must carry out a survey of the views of the population. This is neither a referendum nor a plebiscite; unlike in elections, voting is voluntary, and the results are non-binding. Yet the state budgets $122 million for its opinion poll, which is to be preceded by a 'balanced' debate. Public money is handed in equal parts to campaigns for and against same-sex marriage. The adverts hit prime-time family-hour television and high-school English classes. They are on the radio in the morning and the timeline feed at night.

Twelve million and seven hundred thousand people fill out a form and post it back. It asks:

Should the law be changed to allow same-sex couples to marry?

[ ] Yes   [ ] No

Footy Season, 2019

All the footy dykes are engaged. I know because they post about it everywhere and because I still have channels for enquiring about the drama that oozes from every update. The couples share rings and grins and pictures where they look alarmingly like one another. I look for clues in the backdrops of the places—microbreweries and wine country—where they decide to make themselves mean something to the state. Let's just say the home-ownership announcements are never far off.

In the season we played together, I had a lot of fun and built up my tolerance for shit-tier beer. I was constantly amazed at how far everyone took being a Team into their daily lives. I still think it was one of my few experiences of proper community. At the same time, the scene was pretty white and I never fully let my guard down, having grown up suspicious of Australian football culture. We had a good time, though, and I would have stuck with it if I hadn't moved away. I play football (soccer) with a queer team in London now; the ball is round, I am less afraid of head injuries and no one has plans to get married.

15 November 2017 (A.M.)

I wait tables at a chain café for the better part of two years. The shop is nestled in an arcade on the high street of the wealthy neighbourhood where we grew up. That morning, I tram in the dark from my parents' place to lay out industrially prepared pastries under expensive lighting. The opening hour passes in silence before our regular clientele arrive—an array of the oldest, whitest and most entitled residents of Melbourne's eastern suburbs. At the counter, they take care to enunciate their orders clearly for the sake of our mostly brown staff. I then bring (extra-hot) lattes and overpriced croques monsieur to their tables as they pore over Murdoch tabloids. Ten o'clock beckons as I inch toward the end of the early-morning shift, my phone a ticking time-bomb in my pocket.

I am still in uniform when the plebiscite results are released.

61.6 per cent. I stand on the street and let the automatic doors glitch behind me. 61.6 per cent. My head swims to make sense of the figure and arrives at its natural companion: 38.4 per cent. I am thinking of the room full of people behind me, the people I woke up early to serve. I am wondering how many of the cups of coffee and plates of food that I have laid out today were taken by someone who went out of their way to say *No* to us. I tram home to strip off the beige-brown garb and the sickly-sweet smell it absorbs. My friends are in town already. I am soon on my way.

27 June 1992/2022, 4 July 1992/2022

My parents marry twice—a white church wedding and a brown community-centre wedding—and mark both occasions every year. They are in London to visit me when the two tricennials pass, so I join them as they celebrate their fifty-ninth and sixtieth anniversaries. It is painfully clear, across a dimly lit dinner table, why all three of their kids turned out to be simps.

2013–

After we meet a real-life teenage dyke for the first time, a friend says *I know you're not straight, but like, how much?* I explain that I'm all-the-way-gay with the weak exception of my long-term fabricated man-crush. It then only takes a couple of days to do away with him. Over the years that follow, a lot of other real-life teenage dykes come into my life. We all agree that it's one thing to realise you like women and another to realise you don't like men. The revelations happen at different intervals and carry different weights for each of us. Mine was narrow, light and loosely documented in a top-secret Moleskine journal. In retrospect, the lack of attention I got from boys put me on the fast track to dyke actualisation. It became apparent very quickly that all I had to lose was an out-of-focus fantasy. Once I let it go, the world was crisp.

Too soon

I am left to interpolate a suicide from the links on a Facebook obituary.

24 February 2022

Having returned from a wild goose chase behind the bar, Dad wants to understand more about gay sex. We tag-team our takes on the erotics of sameness until he starts to get the point: that desire is as much about dynamics as it is about subjects and objects; that no one does their reaching in a vacuum. I don't know why the conversation turns to shame (maybe shame turns to us?), but the world-weary trace of my best friend's Catholic schooling pulls up a chair at our table.

It is here that I see what I do not have and feel the levity of never having had it. There is something personal, generational and probably kind of Protestant about the unremarkableness of my coming out. The realisation came to me as a simple truth, not a question of right or wrong. I recall feeling shock, fear, confusion and excitement. Shame was out of the question.

2010–2016

[ ] logs on to let me know she wants to die.

[ ] has a question after chemistry.

[ ] makes a new burner account every three weeks.

[ ] starts passing notes when we are eleven.

[ ] and [ ] message separately about their first kiss.

[ ] sends death threats first and love declarations second.

[ ] says she'll jump unless I kiss her.
(I don't, nor does she.)

[ ] is still closeted when we meet with the vice principal.

[ ]'s parents get a call from the counsellor.

[ ] couldn't say it to my face.

[ ] DMs three years later to say she got out in time.

26 August 2017

It's become something of a chore at this point, which is really pretty sad. It goes: Melbourne Central escalators—State Library Lawn—rainbow-flag capes—blue-haired tween—dyke mums of Staffy—dyke mums of Greyhound—dyke mums of children—inaudible speeches—swerve a Marxist newspaper—kids in school uniform—teachers' union banner—old-monied fags—law students in hi-vis vests—there goes the organ harvesting petition—amble down the tram tracks—past the GAY-TM—past the YES in shop windows—lanyard on lunch-break—rainbow-flag cops—hear a half-hearted chant—spot the slogan poster—thinking *is it really love?*—that dog has a jacket—*or is it something else?*—then we're home before dinner—then we're off for a drink—barely even grown—watch it shrinking on TV—there is no secret agenda—consenting adults only—not the kids who are killing themselves—not the kids in conversion—not the kids on the waitlist—LOVE IS LOVE IS LOVE IS LOVE—

until it's not.

September–October 2017

The ballot papers arrive in the mail and we take them upstairs. I hold mine for a moment, then give it to Mum to fill out for me. Somehow I can't face the little 'Yes' and 'No' boxes. What I suspected then, and now know for sure, is that every box you tick comes back to haunt you. I have always had small handwriting, but I wonder how small I would have to write inside the square to say that:

1.   Marriage is a property relation.
2.   I seek to bamboozle the state.
3.   Maybe one day for a European passport.
4.   You don't need to be married to be/have a wife.
5.   There's something kind of hot about divorce.
6.   The family is high up on any good abolition agenda.
7.   Elie Saab chiffon still traipses through my dreams.
8.   The kids will not be all right.
9.   I was grateful to come out in the age of gay wrongs.
10.   None of us will ever forgive this.

16 October 2016

I want to give high-school graduation a miss but Mum promises to *have a word* with the principal if we go. Dad smuggles in champagne and the night is a laugh. At the end of the evening, Mum is there across the room, looming over this tiny old woman, well and truly *having a word.*

In the car home I want to know what she said. She had looked up statistics about queer kids and suicide risk. She told her *if you don't change something here, you'll have blood on your hands soon enough.*

24 January 2022

I am back in Melbourne for the first time since moving away and my parents want to talk about the past. Mum tells me she mourned a life I wouldn't live, that she did so for much longer than I knew. She is out there like a phantom, this other me, lilting with the gait that I slammed shut. She has a different way of filling up the outlines we inhabit, of glancing over her shoulder and leaving a room. I realise Mum knew her better than I did, though I can't say I ever knew her well. It is in her loving memory that Mum points to the space where I now stand and tells me she once thought it empty.

But the heat in my cheeks says otherwise. I feel the swell of frayed muscle memories pass through, lift me up and set me down. From the other side of the nervous rush, I am not interested in reproach. I just need her to know that I mourned harder, sooner, and completely alone. That it was my loss to grieve before it was hers. That in the space that it left, where we both saw nothing, I found what makes life worth living.

9 December 2017

The Marriage Amendment (Definition and Religious Free-doms) Act 2017 passes in the Senate with forty-three votes in favour, twelve against, seventeen abstentions and (later) royal assent.

In the weeks and months that follow the postal survey result, everyone is talking about migrants. Every infographic points to an uncomfortable truth: that people born overseas were more likely to vote 'No'. It seems that 38.4 has a foreign face. There is outrage about the fact, and there is outrage about the outrage about the fact, and there is confusion about the veracity of the fact, and no one is really sure what to do. Lots of reasons are given, very few of which account for the absolute failure of the 'Yes' campaign to reach beyond linguistic, religious and cultural barriers, or the horrifying success of the far right at infiltrating ghettoised migrant communities. Let's just say that only one side thought to translate 'a grave to the family bloodline' into Mandarin. I wonder what they're up to now.

15 November 2017 (P.M.)

We don't have much to say to each other, so we come up with a mantra that captures the absurdity of the day: *EQUALITY IS LEGAL!* People like us polka-dot the inner-city parklands. We get a slab of cider from Dan Murphy's and get busy getting drunk. Later, we flock for a mass migration to the best BYO spots in Chinatown. I don't recall what we order, but the restaurant has mirrors on the walls, so it looks like there are twice as many of us as there are. Night falls as we arrive at the street party in Carlton. Sar reassures me, eighteen and anxious, that we aren't gonna get done for open carry. In line at the edge of the sectioned-off road, we complain about the number of cops as a pair of older dykes hand out lukewarm beers. Once we finally get in the air is electric—politically, sexually, meteorologically—with a sense of arrival. Here we are at the end of it all, at the gut-wrenching anti-climax. We speak to the crowd in an unknown language and the crowd speaks back to us. We say *61.6?* and they say *38.4*. We say *what now?* and they say *who knows*. This is not a 'LOVE IS LOVE' love. We laugh and cry and dance on hay bales. We carry on as it starts to pour. When the party ends at 10 P.M., we are shitfaced with nowhere to go.

2 July 2019

I don't know if it is deliberate or a miracle of language, but the first time she asks me to marry her, she says *would you* instead of *will you.* Thankful for the smallest grace, I say *I would, but …*

STONE

A familiar face. We pass through the square and I am
so happy to see him. Hung, both wrists limp, one knee

cocked suggestively; that's how we like it. His mother watches
us scale the cliff from an insurmountable height.

She fixes her gaze on her son and his witnesses.
With a look, she wills both to stand straight.

Jesus will stay in that village forever as rain runs its hands
down his braided body. Stone flesh wears love stains like medals.

For a little while, I adapt the age-old question of the devout and
undecided as a test of my own personal continuity:

    What Would I Do?

A chisel bites down, takes the answer in its teeth.

I hold myself like wet clay, dense and thumb-ready,
and fantasise about throwing the mass against a wall.

What a satisfying sound! I am constantly chasing catharsis.
The word itself drips of God Talk: 'to purify, to purge'; and

still the holy-cum-self-help doctrine of 'better out than in'
cannot speak for my want to hurl and be hurled.

All the faggots in my life love God, but do not fear him.

As for action, there is nothing less cathartic than the doubled-down hotness of raising and lowering an unreliable arm.

WWID? Imagine the heft and the thud; and let that be enough.

LOVEWAYS

Love is Pain

Sixteen and six months in. I knead the feeling into form until it's springy to touch, rising imperceptibly. My heart makes a racket while we sit there in silence. I want to know if she can hear, then she wants to know what's wrong. I want to tell her I love her—so I do. We lay a while longer to stew in it, this being in love that is suddenly real. She swims languid across the room, growing smaller with each stroke, and settles like a sigh by the window. Love, desiccated, is no longer in the air, but has quietly collapsed to lay a rug beneath our feet. Grounded, she tells me what happened to her.

Before then, or after, or at the same time, we make a pact to call it off if things get too much. If we can no longer bear our own or compounded burdens, we owe it to each other to say so. Yet our love bends with time to hold the superlative. If it is as real as it feels, it will exceed, supersede, overrule—and so it does throughout our years together. This is how I come to understand that the value of love is measured by what it can overcome. It is appraised as the sum of what we give up, the weight of what we endure. *I love you even though it hurts. I love you so much that the hurt doesn't matter.* Pain becomes proof: how strong, the feeling that makes this agony meaningful! This is how an organ becomes an economy, how my heart goes to trade: on a *worth it* basis. I weigh up and pay up the cost of it all. (We were nothing if not expensive.) I come to prize love this way, and take it with me when I leave, and no one on the outside finds it controversial. In fact, they all seem to agree: nothing worth having comes easy.

Love is Righteous

In the States, 12 June is known as Loving Day after the 1967 Supreme Court decision *Loving vs. Virginia*, which struck down the last remaining laws against interracial marriage. Celebrations take place on this date all across the nation. Happy faces and hashtags shout the redemptive power of love, declare its triumph over racism. A lot of interracial couples choose 12 June to get married. Every year, a host of weddings arrange themselves under the auspices of Loving Day, investing each betrothal with another performative dimension: 'I hereby pronounce you white and not. You may now miscegenate with pride!' As a believer in both the very real matter of race and its total, indefensible absurdity, I find couples who lean into racial difference just as unnerving as those who deny it. I find it hard to understand the desire to make a marriage about the history of its impasse. In fact, I find it hard to understand the desire to make a marriage at all. But when it comes to Loving Day celebrants, what I really want to know is what they seek to prove, and for whom.

Love is Love

I have a dead future in my memory. A tall, non-threatening, non-descript man would one day stand behind me at concerts and write me tasteful love songs. I would wear an Elie Saab gown at our wedding and he would be the charming, easy-going alt-boy complement to my fiery, combative alt-girl adult self. We wouldn't have children or sex, but we would have a beautiful modernist home. Then the man died, and so did his maybe-me wife, and the prospective love songs he might have written never got their hearing. The damage could have been much worse given that, like most fourteen-year-olds, I had not invested too much in the person that each of us, he and I, would be. He died, and I mourned, and the blank slate ahead of me felt very real and very blank for a while.

Then I started to sketch. I didn't know what loving women would be like because I didn't have any indie rom-coms to base my ideals on. I wasn't going to get married because at the time of this untimely death, marrying anyone but my deceased imaginary man was made unthinkable by law. Friends soon joined the project, and we coloured things in with fantasies of communal living. We were going to have a charmingly derelict share-house in the inner northeast where we would be free to bring lovers home and stay up wine-drunk pretty much every night until we died. I browsed real-estate listings instead of doing chemistry homework. Our DMs were alive with little promises, many of which would later come to fruition. I spent a lot of time online, incubating this emergent life and meeting people like myself, including my first love, who lent insight to my drafts. It might sound silly or trivial, but something vital to my politics was born in this period. I learned that every gap was also an opening. There were other possible lives, and people out there who would love to live them with me.

This time was always also lonely. As my first romance coincided with the worst years of conflict between us, Mum mourned this dead future too. Now that she has seen me well in a fulfilling relationship, her grief feels far away and long forgotten. Nonetheless, she once believed that I would never be happy in love. Come to think of it, so did I.

Love is Everything

The last five years incubate another kind of love. A shift occurs the first time she comes back to see me. We just know. And yet the line runs on loop: *I can't believe* ... I know but can't believe, I suppose. The impossible has just become true. It is there, beaming, in the space behind her ear, in each expiring afternoon passed in her orbit. We pile our shoulders high on top of one another to wade through body-temperature streets. I say it time and again as though pleading. So it goes, the whole citric summer. Break through with a thumbnail, peel the skin off in one piece. She pummels a lime so the leakage can take her home. I scan a minor revelation at the self-serve checkout and marvel *how simple, a segmented life*.

Later, the first time I go to visit her, it all plays back, only this time inside out. We are several millimetres above the pavement, bounding, when the shortest night of the year cleaves her open. She stops to unspool in a new semantic gap. We talk it out as Emilie smokes, then follow the music, follow the vendors of individual beers and cram into the home of no one we know well. Her voice is a thrumming promise. It insists across the room from the confines of a different conversation, and I can't stop smiling, all too miraculous. There is time for one more arrival in the last streak of dark—at the home of someone she knows well. Silence falls. A hundred terracotta chimneys crescendo with the dawn. We stand to take a sip of the second longest day.

Love is Soft

I am hardening. Some thoughts calcify on the spot. Harking back to a time of real flow makes it hit just how hard I've become. I want to cry teenage tears, delicious and insatiable. There was a time when I gave everything to emotion in the belief that it is right to be moved, to be sensitive, to react and cut loose. Are you there, belief? Are you hiding? At some point things soundlessly ground to a halt. No cups: my blood runs dry.

The water table is dusted in silt crumbs. Islands of limescale cling to the edge of a mug. I used to be shocked by hard water. I used to think the kettle was shedding its skin. For a liquid to bite, for it to sting and crunch and cake, should not be possible, and yet chalky hair and scum in the basin beg to differ. Once a month I use cream cleaner to buff away the mineral traces and then celebrate the gleaming stainless steel, cold and proud, and think *isn't a dry sink beautiful!*

◎

Love is Blind

There was conflict, overt and implicit, surrounding my parents' union. Trying to uncover the real story is a bit like putting together the jigsaw-puzzle version of an abstract painting. In the end, there are too many pieces lost to death, movement and lapses in memory for a picture to present itself to me. That doesn't prevent me from occasionally picking them up and matching the contour of their outlines. One generation's defiant individualism slots in next to the previous one's heartbreak, each a perfect complement to the other. The sharp lines of class aspirations and 'post-racial' delusions, new and native conservatisms, frame their romance in four corners. Yet the middle is a muddle. Who can say where the problem lay, or whether their love found an answer. For better or for worse, they turned their backs on the stakes. They felt they had nothing to prove.

Love is All Around

In those six months, as the world begs for breath, I feel the edges of what we share come close around my elbows. Motionless, I tune into a brittle song. Like ringing ears, like fingers round a wine glass, it tells me all about the loudness of an empty space. I hold still and watch as she raises a toast, slamming crystal with her spoon without a crack. The resonance ends, unannounced. As laughter tears her weeping face to bits, I clamber in and rest, sick with relief, ready to yield. She is conscious of new lines etched on her cheeks as of late and I cannot understand it for my love. No serum smooths out catachresis. We have lived there, in the elastic arc of her smile; the folds are living proof, proof of living.

Today, I can say my elbows swing as though I'm Dick Van Dyke on a smoky Victorian rooftop. I feel old constraints extend themselves to catch what I throw. I feel the godsend of our capacity. Do you think the poets feel my gratitude? Does she? When I decide to let the soft animal of my body love what it loves, I find it curled up in her bed. See, I am learning to lean. My back grows an appetite for pressure. The walls in here have textures I barely know, prickly and swollen and raw. Love is not what fills the room. It's the door that lets us out—that lets us in again.

AUBADE FOR
LEVESON STREET

The time for going privately insane is over
and you are at his door like a hungry pet,
footy in hand, need on your breath, set
to tailgate him all deadlock afternoon.

You lot wear the house like a slept-in t-shirt
made soft in the grubbiest communion.
With forty years of slack in the shoulders
it whips you into proper potheads,
dressed to hopscotch through bird
shit and slow-cook the ceiling,
swerve the black mould's gaze and
trust the colour of the floor.

Like this, you make a living room a life:
Bri tells a joke that lands like a seaplane.
Shelby gets down on one knee. But your
single-glazed love will let in the cold—
and so be it. The cold cares to knock.

Why not string up this bead of a planet?
Why not spin it on the axis of your thread??
The world turns and you start the other way,
contented in the conquest of a treadmill.
Days are shrinking. Three quarters through
a rage lap of the North Melbourne oval, with
earth in the air and ice in your chest,

you run into the plenty of forgiveness.
But it is almost time to wake up.
In fact, it is very nearly the time being.
You howl as a pack and it sounds like
hot tears. So it goes, it goes.

CRISIS

I spend my first six months in London in a different room of the same flat where I live now. There are a handful of images from the time that remain intact, immune to the alchemy of memory loss: morning light, a stain on the wall, the geese at Victoria Park. Somewhere amid being horrifically depressed, listening to too many podcasts and finishing up a Zoom degree, I get to know the neighbourhood. This involves spotting the architecture of crisis at every corner. Something like a moral imperative drives me to drink up all the ugly. Because of their ubiquity, failures of the state do not stand out in London. They are firmly embedded in the ground.

On day one in the city, I am spinning out in the Sainsbury's Superstore, wondering what every adult and child within a five-mile radius is doing in the same building at the peak of a pandemic. After six months of having to bisect Paris for Indian groceries, I despair over the range in the international foods aisle, at the fact that everything is cheaper here than at the Asian grocer's on the high street. The Great British Food Desert opens its sparse arms to hand out individually wrapped Kenyan courgettes on special. Government graphs plot the days that cushion my arrival at the dizzying apex of the Delta wave. I get used to the sing-song of sirens in those first few weeks; a tight ring of ambulances girds the Royal London as though they're conducting a séance. They ask: *are you still with us?* I imagine the reply from a breathless chorus, from the backs of wailing vans, from the fear pit of intensive care. It harks back: *for now, for now.* I hear the call and response from around the corner for as long as it stays in the news, which is not long. In the meantime, I give up skateboarding and riding my bike in the rain. Just in case.

Many of us have spent the last few years trying to name the relationship between crisis and normal, to decide what would be an acceptable amount of interplay between the two. We agree that it is most politically astute to declare that 'CRISIS IS THE NEW NORMAL'. New norms, after all, demand more new norms. There is an atmosphere, and we are bound to keep on breathing. Our present ways of taking in oxygen set us up to contradict ourselves. The problem is invisible as much as it is all around. I'm talking about the first moment back in the post-lockdown club when you forgot the air might be poison. It's somewhere in the joy of ordering in food while sick or stoned, in the guilt at having derived joy from the precarity of a food-delivery worker, in the indignance at having felt guilt for an individual choice when the problem is really systemic, in the ethical dead-end/room-temperature pizza that arrives at the end of it all. It's putting organising experience on your CV and taking off your mask because you want to be seen. There's a heatwave in March and you sunbathe on the terrace. It's there when you correct someone's grammar in your head. It's your private annoyance on the rail-replacement bus.

There is something grossly moralistic about our perceptions of (and failures to perceive) new styles of crisis/ordinariness. It has become both necessary and obscene to register catastrophe, to which there will never be an adequate response. It seems most of us are teetering on some kind of edge, waiting to commit to a feeling. Within view is a lot to fight for and a lot to live for, and the very real chance that both will run out. We will do what we can, then wait and see.

It takes four months for the chest pain to properly shift after my third Covid infection. I spend that period having to listen to my body for the first time ever, enraged at what it has to say. In the desperate hours before sleep, after I have woken up unrested, an obstinate weight clings to the inside of my sternum, catching on each breath. A game of strategy starts to take shape. I put each new limit to the test, desperate to build a formula.

$$pressure = \frac{-x(sleep) \pm \sqrt{(caffeine)^2 - 2(tight\ clothes)}}{3(stress) \pm 4(exercise)^{temperature}} + paracetamol$$

Indicators emerge. The triggers and variables shift. Still, nothing is predictable.

Then there is a week where everything gets worse. Come Saturday, I am in the basement bar at work Googling angina-type chest pain and manage to induce the worst panic attack of my life. I don't remember making it upstairs, but I do remember being furious that no one is calling an ambulance when I am obviously going into cardiac arrest. I want to say *three of my relatives are dead from post-Covid heart complications*, or perhaps *I have never been more afraid of my body*, but instead I say nothing because I can't breathe. By the time I am settled outside with cold water and an audience of indifferent homosexuals, I am mostly reassured that I am not about to die. At various points in the eight-hour A&E visit, tearful GP consultation and subsequent five-hour return to emergency, I am notably less convinced. By Thursday I have confirmation that there is nothing wrong with my heart. The doctor at the hospital points to health anxiety and post-viral fatigue. The GP tells me to take it easy and quit my job. Over the course of that week, I relay a list of symptoms and associations to a dozen medical professionals. Each retelling snaps away at the band around my ribcage. Each recitation summons the feeling. Over the phone or humdrum of hospital noise, I sense each practitioner's innate kindness and impatience go to battle as I begin to choke on my words.

Disabled activists and scholars have done a great deal to reckon with the tension between lamenting suffering and victimising sufferers. It's like, pain sucks, but so does being reduced to a vessel of pain by people who claim to support you. To offer a gross simplification, the social model of disability and chronic illness works hard to reframe the 'problem' of accessibility as one of broken systems rather than broken bodies. This approach implies that if every access barrier were removed, 'disability' as a category of experience would be effectively defunct. But what happens to experiences of pain in this worldview? Where do people go to do the real and vital work of grieving lost capacities?

Here is where another question needs to be posed: what role do broken systems play in breaking bodies? Yes, it is crucial that we devise ways of life that are liveable for people with disabilities, but we must also ask how different ways of life inflict debilitation, illness, pain and death onto others. Global systems that combine deprivation and exploitation are central to this concern. They are tools in the uneven distribution of risk; some populations are exposed to concentrated doses of toxicity, injury, precarity and lack to enrich the lives of those few who are sheltered. A cleaner in a hospital inhales carcinogenic products while protecting cancer patients from germs. A farm worker collects pesticides in her womb so that other people's children can eat avocadoes all year. Debilitation is not a fact of life or figure of chance; it is the bread and butter of racial capitalism. When pain for most people is a direct product of empire, profit, war and injustice, why shouldn't its sufferers feel like victims?

There are arguments to be made that pain is always political. And yet sometimes it doesn't mean anything. It enters the room without cause or explanation, without lessons or blame by its side. It is incidental, accidental, erratic, opaque. Pain like this is disorientating because it refuses to point the way. All the rage, grief, frustration, pity, guilt, loneliness and shame that spin in its orbit gain momentum but have nowhere to go. What is to be done with meaningless hurt? Where does it hide when we heal?

I want to sit in this difficult terrain because that is where I am writing from. That is to say, I am writing about a hypothetical—something that could have happened to me but has not yet. The cloud of chronic illness hung over my head for the better part of a year, and in the meantime made me very, very frightened. A lot of ugly feelings flowered in the shadow that it cast. For the duration of my acute long Covid (elements of which linger on), the crushing sensation in my chest was compounded by fear and wrapped up in stiff bandages of guilt. In the back of my head was my best friend's pain, entirely unknowable to me.

No one really knows where it came from or what to do about it; it's unlikely they ever will. Still, Sar relays the torture of a ten-rated migraine over Facebook Messenger and a ten-hour time difference. She sends snapshots of her nervous system turning against her for days at a time, of her ventures as a medical mystery. I can listen and I can care, but it remains abstract in the truest sense: I am not with her in those sensations or those waiting rooms. It is someone else cooling her neck as she throws her guts up, keeping her sane through delirious nights. Datelines, day jobs, shift work and other minor misalignments bisect our channels of communication. We shoot beats back and forth through cyberspace: sometimes rapid-fire, sometimes largo, always syncopated.

When Sar has a migraine, she sends little disclaimers and pictures of her forehead to let me know she is still around, albeit mostly offline. Days will often pass before she reappears, three dots in a speech bubble, to say the pressure in her head has cracked open at last. This is always a strange moment. It's not unlike the send-off for a long-haul flight. After parting ways, you fall into step with the rest of the world, only to be tripped up later by news of your traveller's safe arrival. All this time they have been in flight. All this time she has been in pain. The revelation casts a new colour on the 24–36–48–72 hours just past. *What were you doing? How often did you think of her?* In my head, I project shots of me and her in side-by-side montage scenes to watch the time pass in parallel. Two lives, one metric, two rhythms.

These days, when Sar and I talk, it shows that things are sometimes great and sometimes hard, and I guess that's how it goes for everyone. It turns out that I'm not the only one with hypotheticals. As she speaks, I see the virtual trajectories sail through her head, where things go better or worse than they have gone. There are versions where she is more in pain, more alone, further from the world we used to share. There are also versions where we carry on under all-night strobes and stomp arm in arm around the world. I watch her envision these alternate lives and wonder how they feel to play out over and again. In particular, I wonder what the distance forged by pain must look like from the inside; whether my painlessness makes me seem further from her than her pain makes her seem from me. By the sound of things, she is better at making peace with all of this than I am. In many ways, she has to be.

The version we don't talk about is the one where it happens to me instead. I think it makes sense that we don't—there is something grotesque about throwing *in your place* or *if I were you* around in the face of something as immune to empathy as chronic pain. We don't talk about this version because it is mostly unthinkable. Her suffering is foreign, for now.

Night falls over the Royal London's 'urgent care' facility and I am sobbing uncontrollably for two reasons: firstly because I realise I am afraid of becoming like Sar, and secondly because I hate myself for feeling this way. It's a horrible thing to grip on to and be unable to put down. On one shoulder is the political superego, wretched with disgust at my blatant ableism. On the other is something more acute. I have made someone I love into a worst-case scenario. I feel this should not be forgiven.

Through the health scares and depressive months that enveloped them, I've come to see that most of my anxieties fixate on lost capacity. Alarm bells sound every time my body, mind or circumstances threaten to shrink an imaginary future. At some points, this is a global pandemic nipping slow-hatched plans in the bud. Other times it is smaller than that: a dull conversation leaves me convinced that I've forgotten how to socialise. Some menial task wrings out a whole day's energy. A sadness the colour of my sixteen-year-old brain pins me to the bed, just like before. When the loss hits strong, I miss my previous, more capable self. I miss how much I liked her. I think about periods where trust in my abilities came without effort and realise they were my closest encounters with faith. The recollection drives me mad with envy. I want what she had and am sure I won't have it again. And then it is springtime in London, and I am growing less sure. Something has fallen into place; I assume a quiet optimism. I am ushering a new life in through the back door when the double red line comes back, only different now. Months pass, and still there are rest stops on the stairs up to my room. At night I lie flat as my pulse fills my throat. There is a weight installed on my chest, which says *maybe I'll be here forever.*

On my second visit to A&E, Sar forwards me a paper about health anxiety. I am much calmer this time—things are moving faster and a friend is on the way—but the PDF sends me all the same. I see parts of myself and people I know scattered through its diagrams and descriptions. Most shocking are the links it allows me to draw between patterns I always thought of as contradictions. (Apparently a laissez-faire-cum-wilfully-negligent attitude toward the inner workings of your body can go happily hand in hand with a sense of visceral panic each time it does something strange. Who knew?) Anyway, there are two points it raises that I keep coming back to.

People with health anxiety tend to:

1. Overestimate how bad things will be
2. Underestimate their ability to cope

The other striking thing it raises is the difficulty of letting go of fears that seem to serve you. It is easy to recognise the irrational bent to certain anxious responses. But when we live in crisis, aren't crisis feelings rational? It is pretty much impossible to overestimate how bad climate change, pandemics, recessions, austerity and wars will become in the not-so-distant future. We live in a world that is rapidly losing capacities that generations before us took for granted. In the midst of all this, there are two things I think when I feel at my worst. One of them is *my body is turning against me.* The other is *I am losing my mind.*

Both these thoughts are constructed in the grammar of betrayal. They rest on the conviction that failure is both personal and irredeemable—a conviction I know to be both unfair and untrue. Still, faced with this degree of existential insecurity, I think it's probably quite rational to be fixated, to be

73

hypervigilant in defence of the few things that remain within our individual spheres of influence. We talk about it in terms of building resilience—as people, as societies. We aim to cultivate our ability to resist and recover from disaster.

Yet, obviously, there is a significant gap between my inter-mittent obsessions with library books or fitness and the work that community organisers do to facilitate the sharing of skills and resources in their neighbourhoods. My neurotic habits represent a twisted version of the logic of the safety net. The neoliberal paradigm of resilience says that individuals can fortify their bodies and minds against the threat of impending personal risk and unreliable social systems. Conversely, a radical approach says that when collectives of people work to build robust support networks, each member can face failure of the body or mind without fear of being left behind.

One side effect of mapping someone else's potential bad trajec-tories is that you forget about the raw material of day-to-day life from which every alternative is built. When I am deep in crisis thinking, this is what escapes my notice. My ideas about Sar, about my own unreliable body, get carried away by hypo-theticals, every *what if* tugging my attention further away from each of our realities. Meanwhile, her days play out next to mine from the other side of the world. No number of imagined path-ways can gauge the temperature of her nerves set alight; nor can they anticipate how ridiculous the dog will look in his new coat, or how much comedy we will find in a minor piece of gossip. Nor can they say what the next infection is going to do to me. These are details that only the real world can gift us. I think this is because the ordinary—even when it is a crisis ordi-nary—makes up the essence of what we share, and turning to the ordinary pulls us away from figments, from the terror and consolation they instil. When I step outside the lens of projection, when I look crisis/ordinariness in the eye, I care less how bad things will be because I see how bad they already are. It is hard and it hurts, and yet it always proves richer, more of an opening, than anything I could imagine on my own. And it's the only way I get to see the other side, too: the dynamite, the spectacle, the feats, the lapses, the impossibility and the inevitability of coping.

SONNET

There are years and then there are also years.
    Love, what more is there to say?

Our world is made of corners and we like it
    most of the time. I am awfully well known.

This little history of mutual indentation wakes up
    to be a valley on your cheek. As you go,

You teeter at the doorway and describe (in vivid
    detail) the lesser-known symptoms

Of carbon monoxide poisoning. I am soon left
    alone with your boiler (and alarm). Please,

Let us put our socks in conversation. Let us settle
    into animal sounds. I will fill a whole

Drawer with flatpack remainders and an arsenal
    of ill-fitting Allen keys; you will

Give each of our dinner plates a soapy shiatsu
    while recounting some YouTube dissertation.

(I am most often elsewhere, but the targeted ads
    on my phone are already littered with your

Penchant for soft-spoken women who pluck negative
     energies.) For now—that is, separately—

I think of your hate for most kinds of Birkenstock,
     of your private invitation to need. Of how

We shared the same compartment in a fast-
     revolving door just to flaunt our mastery of

Transition. Love, I see you in traffic. The front
     of my bus wants to kiss the back of yours.

You throw me a glance like a foregone conclusion.
     I follow you all the way home.

QUIZ

The following questionnaire is designed to determine which side the respondent would fight for in an armed class war. For most accurate results, be sure to answer all questions truthfully.

When others ask where you grew up, your answer reveals

    a.   everything they seek to know about your class.
    b.   part of what they seek to know about your class.
    c.   none of what they seek to know about your class.
    d.   none of the above (they don't need to ask).

When others ask what your parents do for a living, you also feel compelled to tell them

    a.   how little they help you out.
    b.   what your grandparents did for a living.
    c.   that they dreamt of something different.
    d.   that they never dreamt of work.

In order to salvage a working-class identity, you have to dig back

    a.   one generation.
    b.   two generations.
    c.   three generations.
    d.   none of the above (your class is self-evident).

When you seek the advice of a doctor, lawyer or accountant, you consult

a.   your parents.
b.   your parents' friends.
c.   your friends' parents.
d.   the internet.

When others ask where you went to school, they find the name

a.   familiar (your school was notoriously bad).
b.   familiar (your school was notoriously good).
c.   unfamiliar (too bad they don't know).
d.   unfamiliar (thank god they don't know).

In your childhood home, you did not talk about money because that would be

a.   unsavoury.
b.   irrelevant.
c.   depressing.
d.   none of the above (you talked about it).

When you grift at the self-service checkout, it is primarily because

a.   you cannot afford your groceries.
b.   you can afford to risk getting caught.
c.   it is morally right to steal from Sainsbury's.
d.   none of the above (you pay).

In a hypothetical revolutionary scenario, you picture yourself being

   a.   part of the masses.
   b.   leader of the masses.
   c.   reformer of the masses.
   d.   lunch.

In your idea of utopia,

   a.   poets are exempt from manual labour.
   b.   every manual labourer is also a poet.
   c.   automation means we all write uninspired poems.
   d.   poetry is finally redundant.

When you tell people that you are broke, what you actually mean is that you are

   a.   financially secure and seeking to be relatable.
   b.   too proud to ask your parents for money right now.
   c.   able to take risks because of your baseline security.
   d.   broke.

The role that debt plays in your life is

   a.   negligible.
   b.   manageable.
   c.   stressful.
   d.   debilitating.

When the crypto market crashed, you were

a. unaffected.
b. devastated.
c. entertained.
d. unaware.

The fact that you are taking a quiz to be sure indicates that

a. neoliberalism has successfully dissolved class consciousness.
b. you are grasping at redemptive possibilities.
c. you are driven by narcissistic curiosity.
d. you will not be on the winning side.

The category 'upper middle class' exists to describe

a. the wealthiest half of the middle class.
b. people who are upper class but don't want to admit it.
c. new-rich migrants with humble beginnings.
d. none of the above (it is meaningless).

Throughout your life, you have primarily depended on the kindness of others for

a. your basic needs to be met.
b. improvements in your quality of life.
c. a foothold on the property ladder.
d. forgiveness.

In your list of political identities, you do not state your class because

a. admitting you have money feels like bragging.
b. your massive class privilege would overshadow the rest.
c. nobody else does.
d. none of the above (you are proud of your class).

Tally your answers by letter:

a.

b.

c.

d.

If your most frequent answer was *a*, *b*, *c*, or *d*, time will tell if you will make it to the frontlines.

III

WEAVE

DECLASSIFIED

As a newly arrived and slightly scruffy brown-skinned bender with a bartending job, I get why people would assume. I myself struggled to read the new rooms I was in. Where I grew up, geography gave everything away; within thirty seconds of a conversation with someone my age in Melbourne, I could have pretty easily built a profile based on familiar cues. Here, however, I was stumped.

British people like to either celebrate or lament the fact that their culture is 'obsessed' with class, much in the same way that Australians still buy into the notion that class matters less in the New World. It's true that the rich kids I grew up with did not generally descend from slave- and or castle-owning aristocracy; their money was fresher, flashier and on the whole less embarrassing.

Hold on, let's shift it here: *our* money was fresher, flashier and on the whole less embarrassing.

Still, there was always a degree of gymnastics involved in defining ourselves as strictly 'upper middle class', no matter how wealthy. For those of us who, like the majority of my secondary-school peers, were somewhere between one and three generations removed from Asian emigration, the opacity of our families' status overseas and the challenges they faced upon arrival in so-called Australia were first-class tickets to economic innocence. We held on to any shred of evidence that our riches were earned recently, against the odds and through honest, hard work. On top of all that, the bubbles we grew up in led many to believe that the way we lived was normal. Sure, we were well off, but there was always someone better off to point to, someone with older, whiter money and the variety of cultural capital our families would never touch.

And that is how we learned to talk about money: we didn't. Private schooling, overseas holidays, beach houses and expensive extra-curriculars were taken-for-granted facts of life. At times, we could see that these were not-quite-normal for some among us, and not-at-all-normal for outsiders, but at no point did that drive us to embrace 'upper-class' consciousness. Despite our riches, none of us were 'rich'.

The kind of wealth I belong to effaces its status by way of (largely untrue) personal hardship narratives, where migration and racism supposedly leave us with nothing and our families have earned their new lot. Queer people's disavowal of class, on the other hand, is harder to pin down. Bad haircuts and second-hand style erase many of the material clues. But beyond that, we make a lot of assumptions that keep class concealed. The biggest one is based on some people's reality: class privilege ceases its drip-feed after your bigoted family has cut you off. Youth homelessness as a result of homophobic and transphobic parents is an issue that cuts across tax brackets. Even when estrangement doesn't leave you in a situation of real poverty, it can present a lot of complications, as broken relationships can keep you from accessing the same resources that once flowed freely. Yet many of us don't face this risk. However much we might fight, move away and complain about the ignorant shit our parents say, personal or cultural disagreement is not the same as being materially abandoned. We still have plush safety nets and enviable inheritances coming our way.

Other assumptions let us off the hook too: we are broke students and starving artists; we work unreliable jobs at antisocial hours; we fill up fifteen-person warehouses (not counting rodents) in working-class neighbourhoods. What slips through the gaps—or rather is allowed to slide out of view—is the fact that not everyone lives through precarity in the same way. Poor and working-class people who have no other choice pay the price by putting their bodies and bank accounts into debt. Rich queer kids, on the other hand, take on precarity because we can afford to. This is a temporary condition for us, comprised of risks taken in the unquestionable knowledge that if we need bailing out, the money is there. Side by side in identity and life-style, you see people with nothing to lose and people for whom the losses at stake are marginal.

It's not hard to find commentary on this issue among queer people these days. Every December comes a new wave of memes about glimpsing your 'broke' rave acquaintance's luxe family home on their Instagram story. The humour we use to point to the persistent evasion of class is consistent with the way we 'check' other kinds of privilege. Within online queer communities, parodic takes like 'I'm not white, I'm nonbinary!' do the rounds, pointing to how one variety of marginalisation is used to obscure separate forms of advantage.

The logic at play here interests me, with its apparent system of equivalences. It is well established in Black feminist critique that the analytical framework of intersectionality has been emptied of meaning through much of its popular use. Rather than showing how oppressive structures interact to exert distinct yet compounding forces on differently affected groups, current applications of the concept flatten out the broader analysis of power, treating each '-ism' as an interchangeable unit of (dis)advantage.

Most often, we see this thinking come through in the 'in bio' list of a person's characteristics—namely race (unless it's white), gender identity (unless it's cis), and medical diagnoses (unless there are none). Neatly lined up, such indices supposedly let us know all about a person and their place in the world.

But I notice they only seem to index the disadvantages. You never see:

> Sophie, 23, London. Brown dyke.
> Pisces sun, Taurus moon, rich parents.

I don't want to play the game of equivalence, not least because I don't believe it's possible to equate how different systems of power affect different types of people. That being said, I can say the following about myself with confidence: Yes, I have been made to suffer because of my race. Yes, homophobia and the policing of my gender have impacted me greatly. And yet, no, none of those factors has shaped my life chances nearly as much as class has. In other words, I benefit from class inequality more than I am harmed by racism, misogyny or homophobia.

This is not a matter of erasure or counterbalance, one card trumping another. It's not about breaking stereotypes, either. The world abounds with rich brown people and rich queer people, telling us plainly enough we are perfectly capable of winning the race of racial capitalism. The reason I believe it worth stating so clearly is to illustrate how little of a person's life is revealed in the sum of their marginalised identifiers. I want to ask what happens to this counterfactual in spaces where proving political vulnerability is made into an imperative.

What I mean to say is that the culture of disclosure behind the 'in bio' list serves neither accountability nor justice. I would even venture to say it inhibits both. Talking about this feels delicate, especially given the ways that 'identity politics' and 'wokeness' are straw-manned by the right, reducing radical critique to a game of petty labels. I am obviously not here to dispute the political need for identification with others and with our shared conditions. Being visible to one another and being vocal about our demands are vital to movements for change. And yet I can't shake the feeling that another Black feminist axiom, 'the personal is political', is being mangled in the push to make our lives intelligible in so few terms. We are led to believe that being who we are is hinged on naming what we are, and that both of these projects are inherently radical.

We encounter this push through a negative framing. Our awareness is attuned to the ways we are kept from being ourselves and have shared language stolen from us. In short, enabling or advantageous forces are deemed irrelevant. These do not inform our identities, because identity is a relational process based on making connections, on the process of identification with others, and the things that make our lives *more* liveable do not drive us into the arms of others. We do not gather around them to devise strategies for survival, and so they do not necessitate community. While white people, cis people, straight people and rich people exist as political classes with common interests that they work collectively to secure, they do not experience these conditions as 'identities' or themselves as 'communities' unless they feel the need to agitate for themselves as such.

Another aspect of our disclosure culture that cannot be ignored is how successfully it has been captured by capitalist mechanisms, especially those that work online. Something changes when you relocate the task of producing your identity to the digital sphere. What perhaps was once a matter of naming your real-life relationships is transformed into a virtual network that gathers and produces information about how people like you connect and behave. Here, the relational quality of identification generates highly valuable, easily harvested data, from which neither you nor your 'community' can expect to profit. This process doesn't just feed off your public profiles and activity; the more digital platforms can secure our trust in privacy, the more we are driven to share with them, albeit under the ruse of intimacy. The dataset of you grows more detailed, more connected, and, as a result, more valuable to private firms.

Larger forces aside, there's also something sinister about the politics of visibility that says we ought to make ourselves known by stating our vulnerabilities. This worldview assumes that vulnerability is not only a sign of virtue and good politics but a necessary precursor to both. By no means am I here to weep for the 'nice [ ] people', whose material interests in sustaining oppression might cost them recognition of their friendliness. The real problem with this logic is twofold. On the more immediate level, it compels said 'nice [ ] people' to conceal their political advantages and play up their disadvantages in a bid to be read as worthy. It's pretty obvious whom that harms and why.

In a less obvious sense, I also think this association between deprivation and goodness plays into politically repressive narratives. Everything from dictatorial regimes to the Bible has told us throughout history that the humble, the poor, the servile and the meek will eventually be rewarded with high regard from authority figures, be they holy or otherwise. As it purports to celebrate the struggles of the oppressed, this 'blessed are the meek' attitude subtly thwarts political imagining. Its message, that you are only as worthy as you are downtrodden, chastises those who long for a better lot, for a world where no one is lacking. Righteousness will cost you everything, and to want more means giving it up.

I know for a fact that, among queer and radical circles, there are plenty of people like me—people who have class privilege and don't know what to do with it. This is not the same as not knowing what to do with actual money, though it is related. I mean that within cultures where we are instructed both to expose ourselves to the maximum and to conceal any details that might taint our political innocence, there is no set script to follow for disclosing wealth. Put crudely: how do you come out as rich?

If I'm losing you here, that's reasonable. I do not expect any poor or working-class person to sustain a shred of empathy for the tribulations of declaring your fortune. Our feelings of awkwardness are not a real burden, and I'm not here to say that it's hard, although I do think we could make it easier by talking about it. On the whole, although it is never comfortable, I find it far less cringe to hear someone speak plainly about their wealth than to watch them do backflips trying to conceal it. The question then regards what these frank conversations involve, where they take place, and who participates. In my experience, breaking down the habits in which we have been trained—evading class while we insist on other oppressions—is an essential part of the process. We need to stop pretending we relate to the struggles our working-class peers endure. We also need to break the cycles of making excuses for our wealth. It does not matter when, by what means and at what personal cost your money came to you, or whether it is yet to land in your generation's bank accounts. What matters is that you and your people have it, and that you have it precisely because (and so that) others do not.

The biggest and most obstructive reason why rich people keep wealth in the closet is because this is where real wealth belongs: hidden and hoarded. In fact, that's most likely how we came to possess it in the first place. When we make our class privilege visible, we are exposing something that is designed to more comfortably remain under wraps—that is to say, more comfortably for us. It is fair to expect that when someone who aligns themselves with anti-capitalist politics exposes their unequal allotment, they are declaring their will to see it redistributed. Those who keep it hidden recognise the fairness of this expectation all too well. With cash, hiding is holding.

I am not encouraging an alternative culture of class-based confession. Just imagine, trust-fund figures and annual school fees in a pinned tweet; an author's net worth and property portfolio printed on the inside cover. No, this is not about redemption-by-reveal. I do not want to buy into the notion that baring all makes us clean-slated heroes, or that truth-telling washes away our sins and complicities. What interests me is a style of transparency that serves real accountability and demands just redistribution. I want us to show our cards so others know what they can expect from us. It is important to stress the dangers involved here, as there are plenty of reasons to suspect that an outed elite of wealthy leftists would wield their money over the people they claim to support. Charity and saviourism have no role to play in the destruction of class-based oppression. The principles of mutual aid and solidarity are better placed to guide: each gives what they can and takes what they need.

At a foundational level, this requires that we treat capitalism as integral to all modern systems of oppression. It hurts all of us, even those for whom its damage is limited to the alienation and inhumanity of depriving others of access to wealth. Appeals to other avenues of justice are hollow when they lack class analysis, when they are not materially anti-capitalist. To obscure class in our discussions of racial, gendered and sexual violence is to foreclose real liberation. That means no more caching our capacities, no more falsifying lack. To my crew-cut comrades and brown-skinned brethren of the modern bourgeoisie: it's time to put our money where our mouths are.

JANIFESTO

Jepigraph

What are jorts, if not jeans persevering?

Jamily

1. stone-grey / mid-rise / bought 2013 / cut soon after / tied at the back / now slung low
2. jet-black / tight-legged / bought 2015 / cut a year later / snug on the hips / retired
3. mid-blue / Jennifer Aniston / bought 2015 / already cut / bin-bag storage
4. mid-blue / from Sydney / bought 2017 / cut 2019 / three major holes / let go
5. dark-blue / pound bin / bought 2022 / three jorters / carpenter loop / at risk
6. acid-wash / front pleats / bought today / cut tomorrow / cuffless / etc.

Joem

january reeks. fruits and upper arms left out to ripen
overnight show up dripping in the morning. from
racerback criss-cross muscle-cut wounds, their nectar
trickles down the backs of your legs, pools in your
socks, stains them sweet.

Jexposed

1.   Deltoid (del- ˌtȯid)

'a large triangular muscle that covers the shoulder joint, serves to raise the arm laterally, arises from the upper anterior part of the outer third of the clavicle and from the acromion and spine of the scapula, and is inserted into the outer side of the middle of the shaft of the humerus'—Merriam-Webster Dictionary

2.   Vastus medialis ('vas-təs- ˌmēd-ē-'ā-ləs)

'the division of the quadriceps muscle that covers the inner anterior aspect of the femur, arises chiefly from the femur and the adjacent intermuscular septum, inserts into the inner border of the patella and into the tendon of the other divisions of the muscle, sends also a tendinous expansion to the capsule of the knee joint, and is closely and in the upper part often inseparably united with the vastus intermedius'—Merriam-Webster Dictionary

Jicons

1.   Bart Simpson in *The Simpsons*, dir. Matt Groening (1989–present)

Simple drawing style means the denim weave of Bart's bottoms can be neither confirmed nor denied. That being said, nobody skates in chinos.

2.   Korben Dallas in *The Fifth Element*, dir. Luc Besson (1992)

During the final showdown, a full suit organically deconstructs around Bruce Willis' heaving muscles until only a white shirt—sleeves torn away—and suspenders remain. Forget about denim; this is combat-induced cut-off. (Special shout-out to JPG and that painted-on orange tank.)

3. Nani Pelekai in *Lilo & Stitch*, dir. Chris Sanders and Dean DeBlois (2002)

Incontrovertible proof that jorts are for hugging big brown thighs and framing belly buttons.

4. Max Sweeney in *The L Word*, dir. Ilene Chaiken (2006–2009)

Baggy jorts were perhaps the only comfortable thing to feature in this entire narrative. Extra credit for the denin camo cap.

5. Nicki Minaj in 'Super Bass' (music video), dir. Sanaa Hamri (2011)

Short jorts that raised more questions than answers—least of all: how did they manage to stay up, unbuttoned, for the entire duration of the song?

Juntouchable

1. giraffe tee / dad bought for / mum's twentieth birthday
2. graduation tee / with mum's first name / and dad's last name / on the back

Jelements

Ph 1		Sb 2
Pit hair		Sunburn

Re 3	Gc 4	Sm 5
Raw edge	Gold chain	Safety-pin mend

Fs 6	Sc 7	Ti 8
Food stain	Scrunching	Tag itch

Dp 9	Ch 10	Ss 11
Darned pocket	Crotch hole	Skateboard scuff

Uc 12		B 13
Uneven cuff		Bloodstain

Jevolt!

We, the discarded sleeves and lower legs of garments new and old, come forth to proclaim our inalienable rights. For too long, we have endured the dogma of cutting-off, cropping and jortification. Today we say: enough! Ne'er hath a sleeve nor bottom half oppressed a snip-happy dyke in the manner we today find ourselves oppressed. The doctrine of 'sun's out, guns out' has gone too far. No more shall we submit to the terror of hair-cum-fabric-cum-hair scissors, wielded without mercy by our unfeeling tormenters. We rise up for the restoration of our integrity. From the pits of bedroom bins to the wasteland of the scrap heap, off-cuts of the world, unite!

GROUNDING

I am freshly nineteen when I pay my first visit. A weeknight organising meeting—the first of its kind that I attend—winds up with plans to head up to the Embassy on Saturday. I volunteer to join. Somebody's relative's SUV careens out of the city in the early morning with our unlikely band in tow, leaving the city as the sun comes up. Two of us without licences give faulty directions as our more qualified comrades head the wrong way through roundabouts and miss exit after exit. The others are older and more experienced in organising than I am, but also kinder and more trusting than they need to be. I feel at ease in their company. For the duration of the ride, I listen in to their conversations, chiming in where I can and drinking up new information. By the time we arrive, this is what I know:

The Djab Wurrung Heritage Protection Embassy was founded in 2018 in response to state government plans to double a highway running through the area. The Western Highway project was first proposed five years earlier with an approved Cultural Heritage Protection Plan in place. However, this plan failed to protect a 12.5-kilometre-long stretch of land between Ararat and Buangor, where 3,000 trees would have to be removed. This region has special significance for the Djab Wurrung people. More specifically, it is sacred Women's Country, and around 200 of the trees marked for removal represent vital cultural sites. Two in particular are central to the fight. One is an 800-year-old Birthing Tree, which has overseen the delivery of over fifty generations in the hollow of its trunk, each placenta buried at its roots. The other is a 350-year-old Directions Tree, which has been manipulated gradually over the centuries to take on a breath-taking whirling shape.

When threat to the trees escalated, a small group of Djab Wurrung leaders established three camps in the area to prevent heavy machinery from accessing the region by all means necessary. A huge range of people come to visit, learn and show support, be it on day trips or for long-term stays. The Embassy has since become a site for community-building and political education. It is a sober space where anyone is welcome to stay, so long as they respect one another and the values of the land defence occupation. Provisions are in place to stage lock-ons and tree-sits if necessary, placing bodies in the line of bulldozers, but for now the ambience around camp is cheerful and relaxed.

There is a difference between works made by Asian diasporic artists and Asian Diaspora Art. The latter is an institution—in cultural and material terms—that absorbs and disciplines a fraction of the former. There are galleries to display it, magazines to commentate on it, prizes for rewarding it and grants that ensure it gets made. The work that inhabits these spaces, the real engine behind the industry, can take on many forms. And yet, amidst the animations, installations, chapbooks, novels, paintings, zines and tapestries, an alarmingly singular ethos begins to take shape. Its rules are as follows:

1. **Look backwards:** Conjure up an unreachable past and revel in its loss. An archival print. A yellowed scrap of fabric. The textures of an inheritance eaten up by time itself. Follow the threads of a bygone era and get to know the ghosts. This is the realm of the spectral, haunting and uncanny elements, strung together by fragments of memory.

2. **Point elsewhere:** The quest for meaning lifts the artist off the ground. From such a dislocated vantage point, disorientated maps and linguistic borderlands spin in and out of view. Of course, there is no home in sight. This is the art of the homeless, the unsettled, the 'third-culture' exiles (with multiple passports) who know where they come from almost as well as they know they are not going back.

If you have not passed time in the institution of Asian Diaspora Art desperately looking for yourself, then, first of all, congratulations! It is perhaps mean-spirited to say, but there is not a great deal to find there. I get what drives us to go looking, and I get why this art exists. The appeal was very much alive to me once; I've done enough embroidering collages, pondering ocular memories and recontextualising faded pictures of my ancestors to understand why we do it. Diaspora melancholy runs deep, and it needs to find an outlet somewhere. Art is an especially cathartic tool for doing the work of making sense— of yourself, of your history and of your place in the world. Its conventions offer up a mirror that frames us in good light, in good company, with our backs firm against the wall.

At the very least, however, when Asian Diaspora Art confines itself to these rules, it begins to grow aesthetically boring. When you start to notice the particular buzzwords and visual cues that populate this scene, you soon realise not only that they are everywhere but that they are also used to gatekeep notions of authenticity. Yes, homogenisation is an issue for any creative movement that gains institutional clout. But none of this would be a problem if it didn't come at the cost of other points of view. The ethos of Asian Diaspora Art urges us to hold a vantage point that excludes the here and now. By prioritising disconnection and discontinuity, it invites a worldview that fetishises a way of being that is dislocated and lagging behind. In other words, presence is never the source of meaning in

Asian Diaspora Art. If anything, presence is obscured. Some-where, beyond the limits of the frame, stand two feet: on the ground.

The thing that strikes me most about driving through regional Victoria is the colour scheme, which hits its monochrome peak in the late summer. For an eye trained on the lush English Pastoral, it proves bitterly resistant to romance. The grass refuses to live past late November. From above, the little patchwork quilt of farmland appears faded and barren, each drought bleaching its fleeting green into a stubborn yellow-brown. Years later, as a heatwave hits England, I'll play football in the dust, and the scent of dead grass and earthy haze will take me back, momentarily, to where gum leaves hang about like smoke, a silver-ash-blue-copper film that penetrates your sinuses and vibrates with the cicadas in the heat.

The transplantation of the geography of 'home' onto colonised space is key to the genocidal settler project of so-called Australia. Fences are erected, trees are felled, streams are diverted, livestock come trampling, entire ecologies are caught in the chokehold of agrarian ideals. In an undergraduate art-history class, I learn that the first invader artists could not paint the world around them. Their attempts to flatten its hues into legible Landscape resulted in constant representational failure; the pictures they sent back to Europe depict scenes in the wrong saturation. Hills roll and trees billow and it has nothing to do with what stood before those painters, opaque to interpretation. Imaginations, not places, are what make environments hostile. So the lens of the Australian Pastoral obscures truth in favour of fantasy.

This fantasy unwinds by the side of the road as we drive, leaving jaded cattle and truck stops in its wake. We pull up to camp with timber, firelighters and other supplies in the boot. We are shown around the different parts of the site before being put to work. I'm thrilled to be trusted with an impact driver and get stuck into helping build a makeshift shed. Later, we use the communal kitchen setup to bulk-cook a meal and sit with the other visitors to eat. It is not until the afternoon that we go to see the Directions Tree, located a short walk away from main camp, up a hill and over some fences. I have never before seen anything like it. I doubt I will again. Tree-hugging, nature-loving, white hippy rhetoric has always given me the ick, and I don't want to relay this impression in terms of its aesthetic beauty, which is undeniable. What happens has more to do with presence. Standing in the shade of the Directions Tree feels like being in church. I say this as someone who has spent a lot of time in churches without ever having religious faith. In both cases, the feeling of reverence is not for a belief that I share in, but for the sense that belief itself is all around, that it knows its own force, that the objects that receive it hold it well. The need for silence is palpable in presences like this; no one has to be shushed or shooed. When you face the Directions Tree, the value invested in it by innumerable others is palpable, radiating back.

I speak of reverence and not romance for a reason. Romance is what we project onto objects, the meaning we inscribe in them, despite them, with awe and adoration. Reverence, on the other hand, is necessarily a way of being in relation. It's a feeling born from the feelings of others, those who gather around and before us. Romanticised objects are fixed in our minds. The things we revere have a power of their own. They exceed our individual knowing.

We leave the Directions Tree and return to camp, where we eat and laugh and listen as one of the leaders of the Embassy project explains what land defence means to him. We sleep in tents and wake with first light. The morning is passed finding ways to be useful before we pack up and head home. In the car back to the city, I watch the ground take on new shapes as it passes beneath us. Leaving the metropolis feels like shedding layers. Coming back, they stack on heavy. When you have glimpsed how much meaning can be embedded in a place, every inch of farmland and suburb and skyscraper that passes by feels like it's sitting on a secret.

In so-called Australia, this is a justified suspicion. The Boon Wurrung country where I passed my daily life was always dense with meaning, however inscrutable it was to me. The city is a lens that cuts its foundations out of focus. If you want to be drawn into place, to encounter its layers, you have to know where to look. At the same time, looking is never enough. 'Country'—a widely used term for Aboriginal and Torres Strait Islander conceptions of being-in-place—is not a script to be dusted off and read by anyone. Even if it were, a settler like me would have no right to do so. To understand Country is to care for it, to nurture it, to relate to it as a dependant. Such a relationship could flourish if it were facilitated by its rightful custodians, but for an outsider to try and will it into existence would be futile, if not actively destructive.

The Embassy became a place where encounters with Country were facilitated within and beyond the Djab Wurrung community. Outsiders came to witness a small fraction of what the sacred sites could mean to those who had cared for them since time immemorial, all while forging our own relationships with the site and its occupants. This is how we came to care and to act on that caring, how we underwent minor initiations into an anti-colonial ethic that sustains people in place as dependants rather than owners. This is why, when the alarm was raised, we answered the call from camp.

Visual culture, and especially that which calls itself political, teaches us how to look. Much in the same way that narrative teaches us how to story the world around us, the aesthetic codes we consume train us to interpret what we see. We adopt the artist's point of view, heeding the cues they teach us to recognise, gleaning delight and terror from our surrounds.

In another time and place, Dad frequents the back-alley gallery, high suburban fences on either side framing his walk to primary school. He scurries, unappreciative, past Hounslow's latest masterpiece:

> **PAKIS GO HOME**
> (1970–?)
> Artist unknown
> Spray paint on treated pine

This, too, is Asian Diaspora Art, albeit of a different kind.

The next drive up to the Embassy is shrouded by the aura of emergency. There is no time for truck-stop driving lessons or woeful navigation. Heavy machinery has been spotted in the area. This is the day we were waiting for. Roadblocks stop us from getting too close to camp, so we disrupt a herd of cattle and traverse a field on foot. There is a nervous quiet among the masses of us who have piled up from the city in the early hours.

Everyone wants to be useful. In small groups, we calculate our personal capacities for risk. The party is divided into arrestable and non-arrestable bodies who will respectively get more or less in the way.

No arrests are made in the end; the day is mostly comprised of standing about looking staunch. Still, there is something eerie about riot cops on a dirt road, sweating behind sunglasses and navy-blue armour. Dust and insects thicken the air. I have never seen them look more antagonistic. Among the pink-faced, capped and sunglassed battalion is an East Asian guy in uniform. One of the camp leaders, a Djab Wurrung man, begins to jeer at him. Things get personal. People in the group seem unsure what to make of it—a Blak land defender taunting an Asian cop for having sided with the colonisers. It's uncomfortable, but what he's saying is true. The same thing has happened in all of our countries; *the white man*—his white colleagues—will never truly respect us.

Eventually, the police are ordered to leave, and we chase their reversing vehicles back down the road, singing and shouting as we go. There is relief in the air, but also an unnerving consensus that this is far from over. Legal defences and court appeals against the highway construction are wearing thin. Authorities are getting more aggressive and more strategic in their attempts to infiltrate the site with their machinery. We may have won this battle, but the war wages on.

Diaspora is a messy concept. At the first degree it means the spreading of seed. Picture it: one generation is scattered in the wind and the next finds nutrients, sprouts and roots. You could fill libraries with books about diaspora consciousness and its trickster offspring. People like us see the world askant—or so it goes—and our angles of perception are as much a gift as they are a strain. You could also fill libraries with the critique of these notions in line with what I have expressed already. Where is the scope for a situated, future-orientated politics among a people fixated on a distant past? This is especially pressing in settler-colonial contexts, where for non-Indigenous people, regardless of their origins, there is no uncomplicated or innocent way to occupy stolen land. Upon my return to London in 2021 after years spent trying to tune my ethical compass to the standpoint of an unauthorised occupant, it felt strange to live in a place where I felt a real sense of entitlement to be.

One theory of diaspora that I do find useful is Avtar Brah's idea of 'diaspora space'. Brah spent years studying the intricate weave of social life in the new multicultural British working class of the 1970s. In her book *Cartographies of Diaspora: Contesting Identities*, she argues that not only do the cultures of new arrivals adapt and take on hybrid forms, but the cultures of the places where they land are similarly transformed.[4] The sights are all around. Across the city from the suburbs where my dad was raised to fear a St George's Cross, I see Bangladeshi families in England football kits hanging the same flag from their balconies. The 'daily quote' boards at Whitechapel station feature proverbs from the Qur'an, and it's a brown man leading Jack the Ripper tours with his shining Cockney ramble. Herein lies the trembling hyphen, the unruly qualifier that makes us 'British Asians', that makes Britain Asian. Like the city's own patchwork of ruins, red brick and skyscrapers, the culture that lives here is piecemeal and fragmented, a stitched-up wound that is always bursting open and scabbing over.

Maybe it's because our arrivals here are lesser moral quandaries, but the complexity of being 'in but not of' London seems easier to lean into than what diasporic settlers in so-called Australia face. Even that idea—a diasporic settler—seems impossible. How can people always halfway out the door see themselves as 'settled'? The term 'settler' is itself disputed for the way it euphemises the violence of ongoing conquest, genocide and occupation under colonial regimes. Regardless, like the theory of diaspora space, the notion of a diasporic settler forces us to reckon with the fact that by virtue of being where we are, we make a mark on and are marked by the places we inhabit. Our arrivals come with baggage, and no degree of alienation or melancholy will change that. In so-called Australia, however complex that mark may be, a meaningful part of it necessarily involves the stain of occupation.

It's hard to say what is at stake in 'diasporic settler' identity claims. Recognising yourself as a beneficiary of colonisation may seem like the logical first step to making reparations. And yet in many ways, it can stand in the way. As Eve Tuck and K. Wayne Yang note in their paper 'Decolonization is not a metaphor', settlers deploy countless strategies to evade the material demands for decolonisation.[5] Acknowledgment and indulgence of guilt can often feature among these 'settler moves to innocence' that stand in the way of returning land and life to Indigenous peoples. In any case, it would be naïve to assume that flipping the switch from 'diaspora consciousness' to 'settler consciousness' would necessarily drive change. Many diasporic Asians in so-called Australia are rewarded for their loyalty to colonial nationalism, albeit under the canny rebrand of multiculturalism. To give up on these rewards would require a genuine political commitment to anti-colonial justice, not just an abstract identity shift. And the diasporic imagination won't get us there either. When the frameworks we use to shape our senses of self, community and political vision alienate us from the people and land around us, they necessarily keep us from being accountable to them.

Where are you from? as statement:

You are not like us you will never be like us you have no right to be here you are an unassimilable alien humanity eludes you why leave behind your natural place you pose a toxic threat here your body is contagion your life will remain marginal our worldviews are antagonistic our differences are insurmountable my freedom needs your disappearance I could not bear to know you nothing good will come of this it's high time you went home.

Where are you from? as question:

Why have you made your way here how did you clamber through what have you carried with you what did you have to leave behind how do you feel those absences do things here serve you as they should did things there do their best for you where did you learn to cultivate what do you hope to plant here who gets to share the harvest how did your passage change you how does it bend your future where are your new entanglements will you extend them for us who holds you when you're sleeping what time is it inside you which wounds need most attention how can we wrap momentum up and cushion your arrival?

The Djab Wurrung Directions Tree was bulldozed by the Victoria State Government on 26 October 2020, three months after I moved away. This event coincided with the announcement that ended Covid-19 lockdowns in the region after many months of strict regulations. Tough lockdown laws had made it impossible for supporters to legally visit the Embassy during this time. In the news, popular approval of the lifted restrictions clouded public displays of grief and rage pouring from the Embassy and its allies.

There was a ban by Djab Wurring leaders on taking or sharing photographs of the Directions Tree while it stood. Soon after it was felled, the ban was lifted. Pictures of the tree standing tall, its limbs whorling all around, began to appear online. Another image, of the dismembered trunk being taken away in the back of a truck, circulated widely at the time. Many gains were made by land defenders as a result of years of relentless legal challenges, campouts and campaigning; with the new road well under construction, other sacred trees surrounding the site have had their protection guaranteed. And yet we have this picture, still, globally available, of desecration, of a body being wrested from its home.

Building accountability frameworks around others is not the same as deference. A politics of deference hands authority and responsibility over to 'more qualified' oppressed people, leaving those in positions of power innocent by way of incapacitation. In contrast, to turn to others in the mode of accountability is to draw your ethical standards from those with whom you seek to be in solidarity and to apply these standards in your own life. The question is not 'are you accountable', but 'to whom are you accountable'. Who makes demands of you? And how do you heed them?

The openings that emerge when we embrace these questions—for success, failure, challenge and growth—are made possible in the context of community. This concerns not only the communities with whom we share common ground but also the ways we commune with the places that sustain us. Such accountability networks have bridged human and non-human agents for millennia already. The sacrifice entailed by entering them is nothing like the risk involved in remaining apart. Though more urgent in the context of colonial occupation, there are specific ethics of care to be continued or devised for every place. Whatever words we want to use, 'diasporic', 'settler' or otherwise, this is what I dream of when I dream of a grounded way of uprooted life, of a politics in place. This is how we come to face one another, where and as we are.

BOUQUET

Soph other Soph picks me up from
the station, her car reeks of jellybean
freshener, we assemble bouquets
under unforgiving light, unbridled
stems stripped back to fall in circles,
she drops me back at the train with
my arrangement and dusk hits the
windows with violence, here I am in
the glass, hurtling and stationary, me
and ugly flowers riding northwest,
delayed, the seat back wants to touch
me but I won't allow it, not like this,
my triceps are promising release, so
I send an email to my therapist and
swap to the tram at Flinders Street,
fifteen later it unleashes us between
lanes, on our knees, metaphorically,
faithful to the green man who says go.

The whole cast is out on Errol Street, boom
mics falling into the shot, I pick up soup
anyway then lay on the bed, the smell of Shelb
gone cold on the sheets, and think about how
this is not my home anymore and won't ever
be again, and thank god for big feelings that
come just in time, Sar is on her way to give me
pinchies, squeeze high-pressure truth from my

palms, Al is stranded on the doorstep though
she doesn't seem too bothered, oh and pinchies
is like round and round the garden like a teddy
bear, except for grownups who are losing their
minds, thank god for that too.

l leave the airport on layover in
Cairns to go sit on the closest beach,
watch the sun come up, pull up my
jeans and wade, was planning on
doing some serious contemplating
but who knows what l think about
in the end, the driver on the way
back has his own names for parrot
species, can tell them all apart
and greets them personally, he
drops me off and l have the worst
coffee ever and wish l were better
at contemplating and/or knowing
when to say no.

In Dusseldorf, talking loudly about
why l am broadly anti-Germany and
feeling racially threatened, unrelated
stances although maybe they ought
not to be, Luke gets me drunk at lunch
and then leaves for the afternoon so l
buy myself some quark and go to the
library, two things that are after all
good about Germany, and think of
more quiz questions that might make
him change his mind re: love, and read

my non-library book, until it's late
enough to find him again, and steal
his lanyard, and go watch some experimental dance so we can talk about it
afterwards, and act exactly as young as
I am.

Manon makes fun of me for spending so
much money on that Swiss army knife,
for getting overexcited in the shop while
she waited outside, and I suppose she
was right to mock, turns out it's illegal to
carry, that locking blade fixed itself right
in my back, anyway it doesn't matter cos I
am my father's child, which is to say that
I may never use my Swiss army knife but
am terribly happy to have one.

Barely there biking
through Weaver's Field,
I rule myself a liability
on two wheels and get
off, hands in the grass,
to find and reread the
Google Doc that says
it's okay to feel unreal,
meanwhile a man walks
by in the throes of song,
what a laugh, the build-
ings are papier mâché,
two- dimensional, I think
where is the set designer

I would like to pass on my
congratulations, except
now daylight's slinking
off and so should I really,
can probably make it
home now, thank you
Google Doc thank you
Sar for writing it thank
you nightfall thank you.

HOOKED

As a matter of routine, my research lands me in front of the kind of document that ought to make your skin crawl. I flip through diagrams of human types arranged by proximity to primates. Doomsday prophets blame families like mine for the collapse of civilisation. In boastful prose, men of 'science' explain that my 'Caucasian' ancestors were made in God's image and that my 'Asiatic' ones were sexually deviant thieves. I rummage through the archives and chew up their bitter theories until their words begin to disintegrate, losing shape but leaving flavours behind. This is how I learn to digest.

Another kind of writing, however, is harder to stomach. Absurd eugenicist theories about the horrors of racial mixing and hybrid degeneracy are easy enough to dismiss, but the hand of eugenics can also be subtler, less crude in its racism. Instead of challenging the very premise that race science can or should exist, a dangerous corrective espouses that 'interracial breeding' produces genetic resilience. Despite the fact that 'race' does not correspond to genetic difference, the myth of hybrid vigour litters centuries of anti-racist rhetoric, blurring the invented line between scientific and cultural knowledge. In literature, science, sociology, politics and public debate, mixed-race people have been portrayed as the healthy, dynamic, well-adjusted and intelligent heroes of racial emancipation since the 1800s. Such representations formed a necessary defence against tropes of the vulnerable white woman, predatory colonised man and tragic mulatto that dominated racist media; their historic role in the fight against slavery, segregation, bordering and anti-miscegenation laws is not lost on me.

What disturbs me is their present-day resonance: the haunt of mixed-race exceptionalism.

There is a very specific narrative about being mixed that dominates Western thinking about race. I say 'narrative' and not 'trope' or 'stereotype' because this is a style of thinking that structures the way we build our life stories. Narrative forms turn us into the protagonists of our own situations, transforming our everyday experiences into coherent, meaningful plots. They allow us to interpret the past and make predictions about the future, all while gradually shaping ideas about who we are and how we relate to others. Put differently, narratives provide us with character briefs and plot outlines that we fill in with the details of our personal lives.

Familiar figures such as star-crossed lovers, unexpected heroes, likeable underdogs and treacherous antagonists all emerge from particular genres of narrative. They tell us whom, and what, to expect. So, what kind of story features a mixed-race lead? The narrative goes like this:

BEGINNING

- A white person and a non-white person love each other so much that racist taboos cannot keep them apart. They cut ties with those who try to separate them to create a new family.
- A child is born who not only enshrines the power of their parents' overcoming but makes colour lines meaningless by embodying their transgression.

MIDDLE

- The child grows up 'lost between worlds'—the (middle- or upper-class) white world of the Western metropolis they inhabit and their non-white parent's diasporic culture, contact with which is usually mediated by grandparents, language barriers, holidays and well-seasoned and/or strong-smelling food.
- Being 'in between' is deeply disorientating. The child is 'not white enough' for their white homeland and 'too white' for their non-white culture. It doesn't help that their visible race—an egalitarian, ambiguous blend of their parents' races—is inscrutable to others. This general malaise provides our point of tension, peaking through adolescence in classic coming-of-age form.
- Working out how to arrive at a secure sense of self requires serious 'navigating' during these formative years. This process is facilitated by one or more of the following ventures: language-learning; overseas travel; the death or sudden proximity of a non-white relative; a racist encounter; fights with family; experimental poetry; political education; art school.

END

- Our mixed-race protagonist has a breakthrough. As it happens, being unmoored from the bounds of race, place and community can set you apart in advantageous ways. The powers that be like that they can have a non-white face on their billboard or their board of directors without having to venture into class or cultural alterity. A well-paid and high-profile opportunity arrives to reassure our lead that they are 'valid', that they are 'enough', and that what they experienced as weaknesses while growing up are, in fact, strengths.

There are lots of details missing here, but if you're interested in uncovering them, I would invite you to engage with almost any form of mixed-race media to fill in the gaps. We appear as heroes of race relations and global citizenship from 2022 Netflix series, 2000s blog posts, 1990s advertising, 1980s popular fiction and 1960s political rhetoric, all the way back to the nineteenth-century Reconstruction era of the United States. Across centuries and continents, the same story reaches for us, and we treasure its warm embrace.

Appeals to a 'post-racial' future, where everyone is an enticing shade of café au lait, have always served contradictory purposes. They are hailed by anti-racists in struggles against real racial violence. They also feed projects of racialised data collection and institutional Diversity, Equity & Inclusion agendas. On a more personal level, these narratives can and do bolster the often precarious self-esteem of mixed-race individuals. I remember the immense relief, gratitude, peace and optimism I felt when I first saw myself in them. Here was a mirror that revalued my deepest insecurities. In its reflection, I saw all of the recognition and reassurance that people like me could not glean from our most intimate relations. This moment of empowerment is especially striking for those who, like myself, do not face major structural barriers to accessing the promises of racial capitalism. A sense of narrative coherency is the final frontier in our self-actualisation, our ticket to success. Once we come to see our difference as desirable, we begin to sell it as such to others and reap unexpected rewards.

Despite its historic anti-racist uses, I would argue that it is only really people like me who are served by this narrative today. That is to say, people for whom racial alienation, more so than racial oppression, is the highest hurdle to leap. This distinction is important because these triumphs are not only separate but often in competition with one another. While tackling the superficial crisis of racial self-esteem for privileged people, the mixed-race narrative is also carrying out another, more sinister kind of work.

When a narrative starts to appear everywhere and gain mass support, it becomes a force in its own right, capable of producing disciplining effects. In other words, the characters and stories described in dominant narratives become blueprints for others to follow. While the mixed-race narrative might have once served to show us that a positive identity was *possible*, today it instructs us that mixed ways of being are *ideal*.

Whiteness is a slippery category. It has rearranged its boundaries time and again, absorbing different populations along the way to secure power across different sites. Whiteness is less a type of racial being than it is a way of being *without race* that becomes coherent through the stigmatisation of others. It functions as the gold standard of humanity: rational, moral, universal, historical and civilised. By contrast, the process of racialisation measures and marks non-white people's deviation from this ideal. Our differences are made into signs of animality, backwardness, stagnation and deviance—proof that we are incapable of knowing or governing ourselves. The process of racialisation fixes this meaning to our bodies in order to justify our death, degradation, displacement and exploitation.

In theory, the post-racial ideal proposes to 'end' whiteness by letting it vanish into 'the mix'. This could mean stopping the process of racialisation altogether. Since whiteness relies on differentiation, it makes sense to assume that it would disappear in a world where everyone was equally 'brown'. But this assumption misses the real function of 'browning' in post-racial fantasy, which is premised on a literal change in skin colour. Notably, this change is already taking place all over the West. As rates of immigration and interracial marriage increase, the white majority really is shrinking in countries like Britain, the US and so-called Australia.

Beyond real demographic change, however, is a subtle shift in the way white people feel about their own whiteness. The internet is rife with examples of white people altering their racial appearance. Celebrities are publicly scolded for 'Black-fishing' one minute and using makeup hacks to mimic East Asian features the next, while clusters of academics and activists are exposed for committing 'ethnic fraud' to gain credibility in their fields. Such deliberate deception is decidedly 'un-woke', but even among the liberals who know this, I think there's a more subtle idea at play: that being white is kind of passé. In an age where it is becoming increasingly difficult to ignore racial violence and privilege, being white is no longer something many white liberals feel comfortable taking comfort in. Of course, this doesn't keep them from doing so, but the anti-racist urge to 'check your privilege' makes many mourn a lost sense of innocence, one that only victims of racism can now claim. Whether we are 'decentring' whiteness in our anti-racist agendas or mocking 'bland', mayonnaise-loving Anglo culture, the (justified) shame and disregard we inflict on white people leaves the liberal ones hungry for an exit strategy. Enter the mixed-race narrative. Not only can white liberals be 'redeemed' by taking brown lovers and making brown babies; they can do so without sacrificing any real power.

As white skin gradually disappears from our census data and our senses of pride, where does whiteness go? In short: nowhere. The endpoint of the mixed-race narrative is, in effect, identical to the post-racial fantasy of an entirely 'brown' nation. In either case, it is assumed that race itself will cease to matter once we move away from the 'black–white binary'. What these narratives conceal is how whiteness as a function of *being without race* continues to operate in supposedly 'post-racial' contexts. That is to say, 'brown' will become the new white, insofar as it will be understood as a 'raceless' state. Racial power will remain, albeit in disguise, because the idea of living a life unmarked by race is only valuable when the mark of race is kept intact, displaced onto others, not destroyed. The model of freedom in the mixed-race narrative is thus a relative one: at its root, it demands the unfreedom of others.

The 'brown' ideal exerts two kinds of pressure on those who do not already meet it. The first urges conformity with its demands. The second is more insidious. Those who either cannot or do not seek to conform are not only punished for their non-conformity but told that their non-conformity represents a personal failing. Exclusion and oppression become the fault of the excluded and the oppressed. In concrete terms, this is evident in situations where Black and Indigenous people with partially white ancestry are vilified for identifying as Black or Indigenous rather than as mixed-race. When we consider the violent histories of enslavement, forced labour, rape and sexual violence, land theft, displacement, prohibitions of marriage, segregation, legal non-personhood, 'one-drop' theories of Blackness, genocidal erasures of Indigeneity, and destruction of colonised kinship systems, it is apparent that there is a great deal more at stake in Black and Indigenous identity claims than any matter of blood percentages or genetic codes. These identities are political commitments as much as they are expressions of personal and collective feeling, and often, if not usually, take on the radical premise that every genealogy is already 'mixed'.

Nonetheless, just as racialised people are told that it is their refusal not to 'see race' that keeps racism alive, those who commit to 'singular' racial identifiers are blamed for their own demonisation. When the mixed-race narrative tells us that mixture is the key to ending racism, Black, brown and Indigenous people who choose to have children with 'racially similar' partners can be accused of harming 'the cause'. This twisted principle states that as good anti-racists, we must desire that our children are less racialised (read: whiter) than us.

Racial capitalism also inflects the plight for a 'post-racial' world. Neoliberal economies demand more and more that we are flexible, adaptive, resilient and agile workers who show an endless capacity to gain new capacities. Those who resist singularity and embrace multiplicity are promised access to the rewards of global plunder. This is the character brief for the mixed-race protagonist. Our experiences of alienation, of fragmentation, of 'bridging' cultures, languages and races, are made into marketable assets. This protagonist is mixed up in such a way as to be racially unreadable. It goes without saying that this requires that whiteness, the 'neutral' and 'neutralising' race, makes up a major part of the mix. They are able-bodied, healthy, attractive, aspirational and inspirational. Most importantly, the star of the mixed-race narrative gets to 'transcend' race because of class privilege, which at least partially protects them from the gravest material weight of racialisation: vulnerability to violence, death and exploitation.

The promise of a 'brown' future challenges whiteness as a characteristic rather than as a system of power, and the mixed-race protagonist is only able to live the 'brown' ideal because others cannot or will not. They are only as futuristic, universal and free as the rest are made to be regressive, particular and constrained. While 'browning' might cut some loose from the shackles of race, they will have already been proximate to whiteness. When your race is seen as neither permanent (as in 'indissoluble' Blackness) nor mutable (as in 'hyper-soluble' Indigeneity), you can envision a place for yourself in a utopic, mixed-up, 'brown' world. And yet all it would take is for a different kind of difference—in class, gender, sexuality or disability, for example—to land you on the bottom rung of your nominally raceless society.

This is what 'browning' does. It offers to change the face of racial power while making its violence both more extreme and harder to name. Our current moment makes this clearer than ever: private schools, parliaments and police forces have never featured more colourful faces. Whiteness no longer relies on white bodies to enact racial violence or expand racial capitalism. In fact, a visibly non-white culprit can often get away with worse.

It is easy enough to say that the 'post-racial' project of 'browning' the West is not anti-racist. But part of its appeal is that it provides a tidy answer to an otherwise burning question: what do we do with racial difference? We can neither hold on to it nor dispose of it easily. The plight of transcendental humanism is cold in the ground. And so long as it continues to impact our lives in very real ways, we cannot fully commit to the premise that race is not 'real'. An inversion of 'browning' logic would say that as more and more people adopt mixed-race identities, the terms of racial difference will become so many and so minute that they will naturally lose meaning. This would explode—rather than collapse—racial categories, producing a million different differences in the place of an idealised sameness. For now, it is impossible to know if such a reframing would actually diverge from the pursuit of uniformity, or whether old divisions would simply evolve into more intricate lines of exclusion.

Regardless, narrating the future of our political causes remains necessary work. Nothing models this more clearly than whiteness, which inscribes its dominance with urgent and expansive creativity. When it comes to an anti-racist agenda, I wonder whether it is even possible to write ourselves into alternative ways of being without bringing the racial status quo along for the ride. What I do know is that we must divest our senses of self and political vision from a story that writes the people we struggle with out of our collective future. Those of us who are mixed enough, 'brown' enough and rich enough to have dreamt alongside the mixed-race narrative must think seriously about whom we leave behind in the reach for 'post-racial' horizons.

MAY

The year our lives shrink and grow more public,
we take to the porch like uncles. I sit in a broken
chair, let my hot coffee cool and sip the draft,

wet with warbles. The same magpie starts coming
back to us daily. We watch his green youth glimmer
from the depths of black feathers and Google which

foods are safe for him to eat.

Drunk men and bagpipes join us in the street,
each trying to make sense of it, the blamelessness.

How some things are impossible until they are not.
How synchronicity has made the world big again.

Sar rides a bike under light like a dream and
I think we'll be okay. Meanwhile, my love and I cash
in on our last 'at least'. We tempt fate and federal

governments when we blow kisses to the camera,
when we catch them. And like that, the novelty runs out.
I sit in a salt bath, the slate walls sweating, and wonder

when I started planning memories, to wave to as they
pass, to tuck away in envelopes. I still brew my coffee
black and miss the bird.

SALVAGE

The first principle of capitalism is the killing of collective ways of life. Entanglements must be unpicked and rerouted, doing away with the networks of care and accountability that otherwise hold us in community and place. The planetary systems of dependency that both precede and include us are overwritten by property relations. Victims of this theft must work to survive having been severed from the means of thriving. Meanwhile, the thieves collect bounties too large to enjoy.

When Marx described this process as 'primitive accumulation', he staged it as the first act of capitalist development, a mere stepping-stone toward economic maturity. The spectacle of global racial capitalism reveals something quite different. The killing is neither complete nor constrained. Its duration and scope sprawl across time and space, swelling with the lifeworlds it subsumes.

SCENE ONE: Unite! at the Disco

A dozen homosexuals walk into a bar and leave with a trade union recognition agreement. After thirteen years of workers rolling through that iconic venue, each gen saying we should soooo unionise, *you will be among those who arrive at the end of a slightly awkward meeting brandishing your boss' signature and an uncontainable sense of triumph.*

You're nervous before your first 'knitting club' session, which is held incognito in a nearby park. You aren't sure if everyone is on the same page and lack knowledge of the technicalities when it comes to forming a union from scratch. And yet the lot of you disband forty-five minutes later, wielding an alarmingly coherent list of values, principles, priorities and demands. Behind every resounding yes and complex disagreement in your meetings is an opportunity for togetherness, and you cherish it. A Google Doc grievance is prepared in time for May Day. The representative from what you all affectionately term your 'parent union' has the manner of a stern but loving schoolteacher with obvious favourites (you) and problem pupils (your employer). At times, you almost pity your boss for being on the receiving end of her disapproval. Almost. You learn how to advocate for yourselves and one another and fight for a platform from which you might do so. At the end of the day, you collectively contend, this place would be nothing without you, the bar staff, keeping things afloat.

It's a strange kind of job. You work there for a year and never come to hate it, which is more than you can say for any other job you've had. On a good night, you feel like part of the party, like part of the community the party is there to serve, and you are there to serve them too, your people, so it feels good. This is a feeling you need more than you like to admit: double-vodka Red Bulls as bonding. On a night where the music is off, or the straight-girl behaviour is especially egregious, you put your head down and push through, making comradely complaints to your colleagues. The late nights are taxing, and your body is subjected to every illness the east London queer scene has to offer, but it's a special place, this bar where you work. Fresh out of a waitressing gig that made you dissociate for six consecutive months, you have been thrust into the middle of a real, connected scene. Every now and again, while dodging buses on your ride up Kingsland Road, you realise you're excited to be on your way there, and it takes a split second just to feel it. Bad workplaces need unions, but so do strange ones.

Once your organising gets going, the wins are so big it is almost unreal. None of you have been through anything like it before, so you come in with high hopes and no expectations. Within three months, you have gained a staff toilet, paid taxis home, new equipment, better welfare policies and genuine cultural change. Momentum slows around the pay negotiation process, but even when things are not actively getting better, you have come together to ensure that they cannot get worse. The clichés are true: there is power in a union. There is also so much more.

Marx mostly describes primitive accumulation in the European context. But although the looting of collective life is a daughter of Europe, her descendants conquered the world. Centuries after the British peasantry were robbed of their share of the commons, colonial powers would systematically destroy the ties of kinship, ecology, sociality and spirituality that supported collective life elsewhere. Even those few places left unscathed by direct dispossession were eventually touched by its ruin; financialisaton, debt, war and the climate crisis feed off the dismemberment of social being everywhere.

Nor is this kind of pillage a one-off event that gives way to regular labour exploitation, as Marx first suggested. New depths are being plundered every day. When there is no more land to tear up, airways, waterways and bodies are targeted. The digital displacement of our social fabric turns our attempts at connectivity into data to be mined. Having taken custody of our material worlds and relations, capital invades our senses of self, divorcing us from any styles of interiority that do not support the extraction of profit.

From this basis, the argument that capital has success-fully incorporated every aspect of human being is convincing. Its ubiquity and fervour are felt all around. I am not sure we can escape this feeling, or that we can find refuge from the substance of its force. And yet I cannot accept its totality.

We are surrounded by the concrete evidence that no theft is absolute. There are lapses left behind, fertile with memory and lively with ghosts. The task is not to excavate or revive; memories and ghosts are not objects of the past but the carrying-on of absences. Do not insult them with accusations of stillness. They move with us, always, gaining and losing matter and momentum in the flow. Memories and ghosts are the raw material of every possible future.

SCENE TWO: Budget General Strike

The first of February 2023 is a budget general strike. You are one of half a million not at work today, because the conditions of work in our present moment do not support any kind of life. As a member of a striking union, you claim to be on strike, although no one's really keeping count of PhD students away from their desks. You arrive at the university before daybreak because the security-staff picket starts early. Over the past few months, they have taken industrial action to demand fair pay and to be brought back in house following years of exploitation by predatory outsourcing companies. The security guards, like the university cleaners, who are planning similar measures, are mostly Black and brown and face racial antagonism that compounds their unfair conditions at work. You were here last year to picket with them and felt exasperated at the lack of support from the academic and student unions. You knew your university had a cold, corporate culture when you chose to apply here, but for a while it managed to exceed expectations.

The atmosphere is a little different today given the scale of the coordinated action. Your plans extend from the early morning well into the day, when a march of teachers, civil servants, transport workers, university staff and people from other sectors will proceed to Westminster. You chat away with members of the security guards' union and do your best to keep warm as MPs and organisers visit the picket to voice their solidarity. The front gates of the university are plastered with banners and signs, which stand in stark contrast to the austere white columns of the main building behind. You ask a representative whether you can put banners on the other side, and she explains that it is reserved for the academic union, the members of which should arrive later on.

Eventually, they do. Academic staff arrive shortly before the security guards head for a tour of the block, so you take off your campaign t-shirt and don a sticker, ready to join your own union's picket. Next to you is a white woman slightly older than you. She identifies herself as a medical research assistant and begins to explain how much her Tory parents disapprove of her striking. Somewhere amidst the polite conversation, she tells you that she hated strikers when she was a student. In fact, she calculated the exact 'cost' to her education—in pounds—that strikes inflicted throughout her degree. You are relieved when the now expanded security group returns from their march, when their noise drowns out her chatter.

Everyone assembles back on the picket line, split vaguely down the middle into pink and red cohorts. The head of the academic union at your university has come to address the striking security staff. He speaks about the crisis faced by workers. He cites the statistics deftly: against the current rate of inflation, the 8 per cent pay rise offered to the transport, postal and academic unions, among others, will actually amount to a 15 per cent pay cut. That means that you, he says, will work twelve months each year and get paid for ten. At this point, you pause to think. Who is the target of this address? As far as you know, the security guards have not received an 8 per cent offer. As far as you know, they have received nothing but contempt from their employer. You wonder if he knows this, if he cares. It is late into the morning by now. You watch as the man who has only just arrived, who

has spent most of his time here lecturing into the megaphone,
explains that he stands with the security guards in their struggle,
before moving on to greet another picket. You wonder if he knows
that this does not have to be a metaphor. That standing with is
something he could do.

Exploring pre-capitalist histories is an important process because it helps to make real that the world we know is impermanent. A great deal of work over a short period of time has built the conditions we often take for granted. And yet we are separated from that past by an irreconcilable distance, largely due to the violence deployed in its destruction. All around: memories and ghosts. Knowing about our pre-capitalist past need not drive us to seek return to previous ways of life. Let it rather be met as a condition of possibility for imagining post-capitalist futures. Likewise, we cannot restrict our frame of reference to irretrievable pre-capitalisms and still unknowable post-capitalisms; we cannot afford to neglect the persistence of not-yet-fully-capitalist ways of being that subsist in the present, both here and elsewhere. This is not to say that anything escapes the reaches of capitalist incorporation completely. Instead, such an approach allows for the coexistence of non-capitalist forms alongside and within capitalist ones, albeit in states of perpetual struggle.

In the UK, the land justice movement represents an organised effort to defend and reclaim collective ways of being, right at the source. By looking to the legacy of the British commons and contemporary ways of defending it, these activists are engaged in struggles on home soil. The public currently has the historic 'right to roam' on only 6 per cent of England. The domination of Britain's arable land by large-scale industrial farming, designed to serve export markets, rules out sustainable, local food production. The majority of arable land is owned by less than 1 per cent of the population, and two thirds of all land is held by an elite 0.36 per cent. In a context where the private ownership of land (and housing) is unattainable for most, groups such as the Landworkers' Alliance, Common Wealth, the People's Land Policy and Land In Our Names are working to expand agro-ecological practices and community-based land management to build local people's capacities to reclaim and benefit from collective ways of life.[6]

✪

SCENE THREE: The Beautiful Game

You don't find the beautiful game; the beautiful game finds you. It has been waiting a while when you stumble upon it one Sunday afternoon, with boots from another footy on your feet and your reluctant girlfriend in tow. It has been biding its sweet time. You could not know it now, but by the time you acquire a taste for metallic mud tinging the back of your throat, its plan is gearing up to accelerate. Every clean pass, every clash of hip and shoulder, every tumble into the grass is a thought-through step in an initiation process followed by many millions before.

The deal is nearly sealed by the time you make it into a stadium. Against what you previously considered to be your intrinsic cynicism, you find yourself flying from your seat at each moment of climax, shouting at professionals who neither hear nor care to hear your commentary. On the pitch, you throw around technical terms like a tipsy foreign-language student at a native speaker's party. The ritual is part of what reels you in. Sundays on the Downs as the days grow short; the post-match pints that loosen your words as your spent legs grow stiff under the table.

Before the game came along, you passed an entire childhood running around in skorts and feeling out of place. The sport your parents chose for you had no real charms of its own, and between the juniors, seniors, club, regional and state teams you represented, you found the same to be true of its players. Beyond lack of appeal, those people put you off. You looked wrong in all the group shots: hairy brown legs interrupting a line, your short back and sides amid matching-ribboned ponytails. The racism and homophobia were never discreet. In the end, after nine years of playing up to six times a week, you left with a hatred of team sports and not a single friend to show for it.

When the time comes to trap you for good, however, the game gives you a team. You know from day one they are yours. A motley crew of not-necessarily-sporty dykes and trans people with no real regard for the rules. Better yet, the group has remarkably sound politics for an informal squad. The game rapidly becomes both your reason and your excuse to enjoy each other's company. Before long, you come to realise that the time you spend together and the habits you share have formed the basis of a feeling that creeps up on you slowly, then pounces. When first describing it to a friend, you begin by saying you have found your bubble, then correct the sardonic framing and say what you really mean, which is that you feel like part of a community. The game fades into the background when you meet your team at parties and pickets, when you prepare care packages and protest banners together. But you know it has a part to play in the love and the camaraderie. They were forged out there, on the turf, after all.

And so now you are in, hook, line and sinker. So much so that when you wake up on match day or roll up to the weekly kickabout, whether the sun is shining or the ground is frozen or sleet whips your naked arms, you cannot help but shout, with only a little irony: IT'S A BEAUTIFUL DAY FOR THE BEAUTIFUL GAME!

The question of salvaging extra-capitalist life is even more complex in the colonised world. If there is one premise I believe to be universally true when it comes to resisting capital, it is that there is no universal way to resist capital. The styles of colonial violence required to instate capitalism are as locally specific as the conditions that preceded its dominion, as those that will blossom in the wake of its collapse. During fourteen years in so-called Australia, I lived on land either that my parents bought from thieves or that I rented from them. The abstraction granted by time and paperwork may have opened a window for innocence, but it fundamentally changed nothing. Settler investment—both material and conceptual—in land as a possession is consistent with continual theft and stands in the way of decolonisation. Understanding decolonisation as 'the return of Indigenous land and life' makes clear that it is an anti-capitalist endeavour because it demands repair for the double-edged damage of colonial racial capitalism's original sin. Again, however, despite its claims and its magnitude, this has always been an incomplete theft; First Nations people all over the settler-colonised world have sustained, salvaged and revitalised practices of relating to land and to community that came before and will continue long after colonial racial capitalism. Though caring for Country is sometimes enshrined in movements and organisations, it necessarily depends on collective, intergenerational practices led by First Nations people. At its core stands a 'custodial ethic'—one grounded in mutual respect and reciprocity, both within and between the (artificially divided) human and natural worlds.[7]

SCENE FOUR: *Agenda Item—Pink Berets*

You are both impressed and a tiny bit disappointed to find that the trope that radical queer political groups are devastatingly disorganised is not completely true. When you raise this after your first meeting, everyone jumps to point out that you have arrived in the aftermath of an intensive period of restructuring in the interest of efficiency and that things are sure to deteriorate soon. Either way, shit gets done here, and after a long while of looking for somewhere to put your energy, it's refreshing to feel useful at last.

Tomorrow, you are going to participate in a mildly 'spiky' action with members of the group. There is something kind of camp about picking out an alias. You have just done it for the first time, and the sensation is not dissimilar to painting on facial hair or putting on a wig. You update your Signal profile and feel extremely mysterious. Rather than being ashamed of your rookie status, you are assured by the group atmosphere that, while the work you are doing concerns serious matters, ridiculousness is not only permitted but encouraged among members. This culture serves having a good time at the pub after meetings, but more importantly it means that the space you share is upheld by very real feelings of trust and welcome. You meet in a freezing warehouse every Monday night to work through a well-devised agenda. It's a thrill and a relief to share a physical space and build a real routine around this group. The whole thing harks back to romantic notions of queer, feminist and anti-racist organising of the past, the ones you yearned for while reading comics and pamphlets from 1980s subcultures. With these traditions backing you, it makes sense, feels so natural, that you should gather like this, that your anger and your joy should find a home in such a gathering.

There really could not be a more demanding time to rally around migrant justice in the UK, so you are kept busy with a wide range of tasks. The border regimes you are here to resist are criss-crossed around the room. A minority of you are migrants, of which a minority are not white, of which a minority are in the tightening grip of the British immigration system. The syntax of your guiding principle—QUEER SOLIDARITY SMASHES BORDERS—arranges itself cautiously around these subdivisions, stringing its composite tensions up from the high ceiling, for those who are looking up to see.

Every capitalist context features different methods of differentiation, and these methods are nothing if not adaptive. They must be analysed scrupulously, constantly. And yet analysis cannot stand in the way of action. Our post-capitalist futures will not be theorised in elite universities or disseminated by global think tanks. They will be devised in the moment, on the ground, by the people who aim to live them together. The fastest way to learn is through mistakes. I am not interested in solutions, because every solution entails a disappearance. What we need are strategies. I am far more excited by moments of supersaturation and sedimentation, by the varieties of current and stillness we encounter in our liquid ways of life. Here in the slurry, composition doesn't matter. We are blowing bubbles to see which way is up.

SCENE FIVE: 'the yes within ourselves'

When you are sixteen, you read Audre Lorde's essay 'Uses of the Erotic: The Erotic as Power', and your virgin mind is blown. It speaks to whatever intensity is broiling in your guts, that thing that is not any one thing but seems to contain the entire scope of humanity, including its rough edges. Lorde's eros, the natural derivative of chaos, is somehow expansive enough to contain all of this. (What a miracle of timing.) Just like that, she rids you of the need to hack the rational free from the emotional, the spiritual from the political. Eros animates all, and your number-one priority is to let it course through you freely, to be animated.

Some years later, it sometimes makes you sad to know you won't access that hotbed of feeling again. It was somehow at once the most devastating and enlivening thing to have crossed your path.

At points in your life when you are numb to the world, you fear
that you have lost it forever. You crave hurt just to touch the inten-
sity. But feeling, much like numbness, is a learned capacity. You
remember it takes practice and quickly get to work. At sixteen, your
concept of eros had more to do with frustration and outpour than
it does to you now. You have known it in subtler forms. You are yet
to know much of its range.

But you feel it in the crowd. The hum of energy that builds on
the first scoping circuit of a dancefloor. The way your joints disap-
pear in the smoke. The meeting of eyes at the seminar, at the rally,
that says everything without giving it away. Eros is the potential
energy of scheming, of organising, of chatting shit, of getting shit
done. When the protest moves as a mass to stop traffic, eros is the
spontaneous arrival of common knowledge at the scene. More and
more these days, you enter rooms full of familiar faces, and eros lets
you all breathe the same air. It is the rhythm to this life that rolls so
deep, you meet it first through the soles of your shoes.

Audre Lorde said: 'in touch with the erotic, I become less willing
to accept powerlessness, or those other supplied states of being
which are not native to me, such as resignation, despair, self-efface-
ment, depression, self-denial.'[8] *So at sixteen, you scavenged for eros,*
drank up every scarce drop, quenched your thirst. You made it your
mission to metabolise love by embracing 'this mode of living and
sensation'.[9] *Today, when you come back to the beat-up volume, the*
smell of its pages sets you alight. You live it now. You sense it.

Once we know which way is up, this thing that we need and
that we're making together is the buoyancy that lifts us to
the surface. It's not Luddism, really, nor is it a pre-modern
hankering. It is as much Marxism or degrowth or post-hu-
manism or decolonisation as it is none of these things at all. If
we start with the shape of what has been stolen from us, if we

begin to sketch an outline, the body of what appears will exceed language altogether.

This thing that we need, it's something we can't always feel without crisp air in our lungs and dirt under our fingernails. Its elements are there when we stake illicit claims—to the earth beneath our feet, to one another—and we sense it still, even when (especially when) they are taken away. Each time we form a picket line, block an eviction, play dead on the street, ground a deportation flight, burn a precinct, plant a garden, squat a building and halt the traffic, it's building in our bellies, heating up. It's the steam let off with our fucking, with our dancing, with our laughter and tears—the steam that forms an atmosphere around us. It's common; in common; the commons. It is the learning that makes our mistakes matter. It's the care that keeps us caring. It has nothing to do with hope, everything to do with doing, a little to do with love. It gives life to unliveable lives and is the *ours* of a yet unthinkable us. This thing that we need, we are finding it, creating it together. There is never enough, but I promise you this: there is always enough to go around.

IN BIO

There are data centres in the Arctic circle. Inside, it sounds like the ocean. Inside, the fans and hard drives pirouette, dancing a song into life. Staff defend their ears against their 96 dB(A) halleluiah, against the loudness of hot air. The immaterial is birthing itself on the floor. There are pictures of the back of your head tied up in the braid of humming wires. Inside, it sounds like breathing. I am looking for the opposite of sound. There are rooms so quiet, I am told, you can hear your organs heave. You can hear the substance of your thinking, the mechanics of your mind, and they say it's like torture, just to hear. The body is all noise. It is birthing itself on your neural network, which we know to be unthinkably loud. There are data centres in the Arctic circle that are modelled on the floor where you are born. Listen out for organs. Deep in the thrum of digital breath and blood, find yourself. There you are!

You will rub up against me to make some static. Every spark is a connection but we cannot touch it at the same time. We will not be touching. We will be points on a plane. I will hold up a high potential interface that lets me see you better, hold it until my arms ache, until there's nothing more to see. You will smell like electricity. As metal warms up in an abstract place, it will fling the smell of you out the ventilation. I will be there, huffing. I will saturate my lungs in the detritus. What pours from here will be ours, or no one's.

Every navigation piled in a stack. Every background blur. All the falling of light, the getting back up. Every imperfect deletion. Every pop-up closed. Every word hurled up by an overfed cursor, every word swallowed back when hunger strikes. Every outline you have taken. Every contour of your voice. Each of its private betrayals. All the freezing. All the time. Each of your consumptions. Every type of underwear. The slumping shoulder, a pinched nerve. Each symptom, hesitation, every drive.

Look at you, you're glowing! There are X's to be marked.

Every crevice of your thumb tip, touching home.

ACKNOWLEDGEMENTS

I would like to thank

Brekhna and Farhaana, whose trust, hard work and vision brought this book to life and built a home for it at Hajar.

my parents, for what they have made possible.

my wife [*sic*], Manon, for the years we share.

Sar, my first and favourite reader.

my friends and co-conspirators, who take me seriously but not too seriously.

all those who have lent ears, hands, kindness and critique to this work along the way.

NOTES

1 After Frank O'Hara.

2 Sara Ahmed, *The Cultural Politics of Emotion*, Edinburgh: Edinburgh University Press, 2014, pp. 7–8.

3 George Orwell, 'Marrakech', in *Collected Essays*, London: Secker and Warburg, 1961, p. 25.

4 Avtar Brah, *Cartographies of Diaspora: Contesting Identities*, London & New York, NY: Routledge, 1996.

5 Eve Tuck & K. Wayne Yang, 'Decolonization is not a metaphor', *Decolonization: Indigeneity, Education & Society*, Vol. 1, No. 1 (2012).

6 Credit for these sources goes to the editors and contributors of *Lumpen* (No. 011, Summer/Autumn 2022). *Lumpen* is a journal for poor and working-class writers working in all different genres. This issue's theme, 'The Land', gives way to thought-provoking and informative pieces on how the ground we're on sustains collective life.

7 Mary Graham, 'Some Thoughts about the Philosophical Underpinnings of Aboriginal Worldviews', *Australian Humanities Review*, No. 45 (2008): 181.

8 Audre Lorde, 'Uses of the Erotic: The Erotic as Power', in *Sister Outsider: Essays and Speeches by Audre Lorde*, Berkeley, CA: Crossing Press, 2007 [1984], p. 58.

9 *Ibid.*, p. 59.